AUTHOR	CLASS
CROSBY, A.G.	E02C RO

TITLE
Hutton

HUTTON: A MILLENNIUM HISTORY

Hutton:
A Millennium History

A.G. CROSBY

Carnegie Publishing Ltd
in association with Hutton Parish Council, 2000

Published by Carnegie Publishing Ltd
Carnegie House, Chatsworth Road
Lancaster LA1 4SL

in association with
Hutton Parish Council

Copyright © Hutton Parish Council, 2000

British Library Cataloguing-in-Publication data
A CIP record for this book is available from the British Library

ISBN 1–85936–081–5

Typeset in Adobe Garamond by Carnegie Publishing
Printed and bound in the UK by
The Cromwell Press, Trowbridge, Wilts

Contents

List of Illustrations

Acknowledgements

The research and writing of this book was commissioned by Hutton Parish Council as part of its commemoration of the millennium. I would like to give my special thanks to the parish councillors and parish clerk, Robert Adams, for their support, encouragement and helpful advice during the preparation of the book. We would also like to make the following acknowledgements for the use of material which appears in the book or for assistance given in its preparation: Mrs Marian Roper, a founder and for many years the secretary of the Hutton Local History and Interest Society; the County Archivist and staff of the Lancashire Record Office, Preston; the County Council Environment Directorate and the staff of the County Sites and Monuments Record, Preston; the Ordnance Survey, for the use of extracts from the 1845 6-inch to 1-mile and 1895 25-inch to 1-mile maps; Myerscough College; and for the following who kindly provided information or loaned photographs for reproduction in the book: Jane Hamby, Sheila Humber, Mavis Lambert, Marian Roper, and Eric Tattersall. All maps and graphs other than those which have already been published elsewhere were drawn for the book by Alan Crosby.

About the author

Alan Crosby is one of the best-known local historians in Lancashire, lecturing and teaching throughout the county and beyond on many aspects of the history of North West England. He is a Fellow of the Royal Historical Society, President of the Lancashire Local History Federation, Honorary Research Fellow in the Universities of Lancaster and Liverpool, and General Editor for the British Association for Local History. He has written many books, including the *History of Preston Guild* (1991), histories of Lancashire (1998) and Cheshire (1996), and *Penwortham in the Past*, the definitive account of Hutton's next-door neighbour, which was published in 1988. He lives in Preston, and his wife Jacquie, is the Assistant County Archivist of Lancashire.

Foreword

Hutton, our village, has clearly seen considerable change over the past century, in common with English rural communities in general. In earlier times the pace of change will have been far slower, but continuous nonetheless.

We are all part of this history and, perhaps like mine, your thoughts will from time to time ponder on more distant times. What sort of lives did our predecessors lead, what did our parish look like in the past, and what have been the influences for change over the centuries? Such curiosity has motivated the Parish Council to commission this village history. What better way, after all, to mark the new millennium?

Alan Crosby has unearthd an amazing amount of information and paints a vivid picture of our village over the past one thousand years. His excellent work provides us with a fascinating insight into the history of a Lancashire village community, and I hope that you will enjoy reading it as much as I have.

John Wilshere
Chairman, Hutton Parish Council

1. The Ancient Landscape

This is the story of Hutton during the past thousand years, a period which covers all of its recorded history. Little is known about the area before the early Middle Ages because, in common with most other places in the district, we have neither written records nor any significant archaeological evidence until after the Norman Conquest. Unless accidental finds or organised excavation should alter this state of affairs the first chapters must always be blank, and only a few general statements can safely be made about the area before the eleventh century. Recent investigations into the early settlement history of the mosses and former wetland areas on the Lancashire plain [1] have confirmed that in the pre-Roman period these districts were extensively settled, and that most of the drier areas along the margins of the mosses show evidence of human occupation dating back to the Bronze Age (about 3000 BC) or even earlier. There is good reason, therefore, to suppose that there was settlement in Hutton five thousand or more years ago. Thereafter, occupation was relatively continuous and, for example, small-scale farming communities certainly existed during the Roman period. The most important elements in the landscape were perhaps the mossland, which covered almost all the eastern half of the later township, and the Ribble estuary. In the prehistoric period the estuary was much wider than it is today, and the sea lapped the foot of the slope at Bottom of Hutton. The reclamation of the marshes and the estuary, by natural processes and human endeavour, has transformed the western part of the township and added many acres to its area. Between the moss and the sea was a belt of drier land, better-suited to arable agriculture and, throughout the recorded history of the township, the site of most of the habitation.

The name 'Hutton' is derived from the Old English *hoh-tun*, which is usually translated as 'settlement on a spur of land' (the literal meaning of *hoh* is Old English, 'heel'). This suggests that the original settlement was around Bottom of Hutton, where the higher land projects into the former estuary between the outflows of the Mill Brook and the Longton

Brook. Today it is still apparent that there is a 'spur' here, but in the past, when the sea came up to Old Grange and to just north of Farrers, this feature was much more noticeable and it gave its name to the settlement. If the 'hoe' or spur was the location of the oldest settlement, other features of the medieval geography of the township fit into place. Cockersand Abbey, which between the early thirteenth century and the Dissolution in 1540 held the manor and most of the land in Hutton, established a large farm and administrative 'headquarters' (a *grange*) at what is now Old Grange. This was probably the site of an earlier medieval manor house, which would make good sense if the oldest area of settlement had been in the vicinity. The implication, therefore, is that the development of the Liverpool Road area, slightly higher up the slope towards the moss, may have been a rather later development, perhaps beginning in the thirteenth century when, as we know from other sources, the population was growing rapidly and new areas of land were brought into cultivation.[2]

2. *Hutton after the Norman Conquest*

Hutton is not mentioned in the Domesday Survey of 1086 – locally, specific mention is made only of Leyland, Penwortham, North Meols, *Argarmeols* (a lost place in Birkdale), and Martin near Burscough. The Domesday record for most of the county is extremely scanty, because this was still a frontier territory and Lancashire itself did not yet exist as a county. In the reign of William the Conqueror it was still divided between Yorkshire (which had a loose control over the lands north of the Ribble) and Cheshire, of which the land south of the Ribble was nominally part. The Domesday Survey is primarily a tax return and a list of Crown assets, and therefore Penwortham, which had a royal manor and castle, is included. The absence of any reference to Hutton does not, therefore, mean that Hutton did not exist, but simply that it was not appropriate or (as with many Lancashire townships) perhaps not even even feasible to record it.[3] In administrative terms Hutton was a township, which in north-west England was the usual administrative division in the medieval period and until the late nineteenth century.

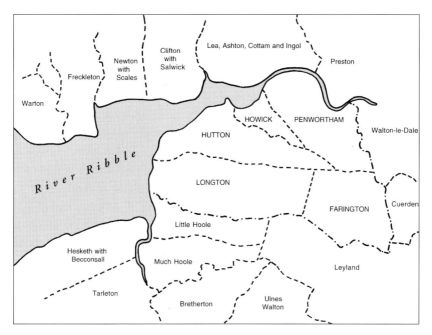

1. Parishes and townships of the Hutton area the map shows the ancient parish of Penwortham with its five constituent townships (before the fourteenth-century Brindle was also within the parish) and the neighbouring townships on both sides of the Ribble estuary. The divisions shown crystallised in the early medieval period and remained largely unaltered until the late nineteenth century.

In the south and midlands each individual community was normally a separate parish, with a church of its own. That pattern did not prevail in the six northern counties and here a parish was typically very large and covered many separate townships, so that one parish church might serve a huge territory. Hutton was for centuries a part of the ecclesiastical parish of Penwortham, one such 'multiple township' parish. Originally Penwortham parish had six townships: Penwortham itself, Howick, Longton, Hutton, Farington and Brindle, though the last-named was quite separate and detached from the remainder. This curious arrangement perhaps reflected an ancient pre-Conquest pattern whereby the parishioners of Penwortham, including Hutton, held and exercised grazing and other rights in the Pennine foothills of Brindle. There were other comparable detached portions of lowland parishes on the upland margins – for example, Kirkham parish included Goosnargh, and Croston parish included Chorley. We can envisage a situation whereby trans-

humance was practised, so that during the early summer the animals
would be driven from the Penwortham area, along recognised routes
through the intervening countryside, and then pastured for the rest of
the summer on the hills before being driven back to the lowlands in
early autumn.[4]

St Mary's church at Penwortham, although most of its fabric is of
the fifteenth century or the 1850s, is a very ancient foundation, and
there is little doubt that it was established long before the Conquest.
No archaeological work has been undertaken on the site but, given that
it was the centre of one of the large ancient parishes of the county, its
early origins are certain. In the Middle Ages the inhabitants of Hutton
perhaps attended the parish church at Penwortham for certain services,
or for ceremonies of baptism and marriage, and they certainly went
there for burial. But, as was the case with most of the great parishes of
Lancashire, there were other places of worship apart from the parish
church. Small chapels were frequently founded in the years after the
Norman Conquest, and one such was at Longton, where a chapel had
been built by the middle of the twelfth century and perhaps earlier. A
Penwortham priory document of about 1150 was witnessed by 'Eafward,
priest of Longton' and there are a few later medieval references to priests
there.

Virtually nothing else is known of this chapel and its medieval existence
is almost undocumented. This problem, too, is identifiable elsewhere in
the county – the chapels were not parochial, did not have beneficed
priests (those with an 'official' income), and left few administrative or
other records. Many were simple one-roomed structures, with one part-
time priest, and they either disappeared by the late fifteenth or early
sixteenth centuries or were later refounded and altered in character.
Nevertheless, the little chapel at Longton, which served a purely local
need, did survive and in 1515 its chaplain was the first founder of what
became Hutton Grammar School. It had no burial ground, as the right
to conduct burials (and thus to monopolise burial fees) was restricted
to the parish church, but it probably satisfied most of the other spiritual
needs of the population of Hutton and Longton. Hutton, indeed, had
its own little chapel, as noted below, but this seems to have been a
more specialised instance, standing on the shore by the ford from Lea
and probably defunct by the fourteenth century.[5]

3. *Cockersand Abbey and its Hutton Estates*

Although so little is known about the early post-Conquest period in Hutton, we are in contrast most fortunate that after about 1200 its history is surprisingly well-documented. This is due entirely to the fact that Hutton's landowners, motivated either by extreme piety or (perhaps more realistically) by a need for heavenly salvation because of their transgressions on earth, gave much of the township to the abbey of Saint Mary at Cockersand. Since monasteries were usually assiduous in their record-keeping, and in the case of Cockersand many records survived the vicissitudes of the Reformation and Dissolution, we have extensive evidence for land acquisition and land ownership. Without the happy survival of this excellent record our knowledge of medieval Hutton would be fragmentary indeed. Cockersand abbey, perched dramatically but uncomfortably on the edge of the sea near the mouth of the Lune, was allegedly founded in about 1184 by a hermit, Hugh Garth, as a religious hospital. It received generous endowments from the county's most important lord, William of Lancaster, and his wife Eloise, and in 1190 became a priory colonised by Premonstratensian[6] monks from Croxton in Leicestershire. It was upgraded to the status of abbey only six years later. The new monastery at Cockersand soon attracted large endowments from landowners and local lords across Lancashire, eventually becoming, after Furness and Whalley, the richest of the county's monasteries. Among its most important estates was Hutton, and the medieval history of this township is dominated by the influence of the abbey, which acquired its lands in Hutton by a long series of gifts and grants methodically carefully recorded in its cartulary, or book of charters. Frustratingly, it is often impossible to identify the exact locations of the lands in question, but it is immediately apparent that here, as is usually the case, the great majority of the properties were acquired early in the life of the house, particularly at beginning of the thirteenth century. Thereafter, secular lords and their families were much less willing to give land to religious houses, partly because monasteries were widely considered to have too much property already and partly because, by alienating land to a religious order, a benefactor effectively deprived his descendants of their inheritance.

The often very detailed recitations of land ownership given in the Cockersand documents allow us to reconstruct the history of some estates in Hutton from the mid-twelfth century, sometime around the year 1150. The record begins with a landowner called Orme de Hutton, who held about two-thirds of the township, the remaining one-third being held by another landowner, Waldeve de Ulverston. Orme had other properties, including lands in Heaton near Lancaster which he leased from a lord called Ranulf de Marsey. Scattered estates of this sort were

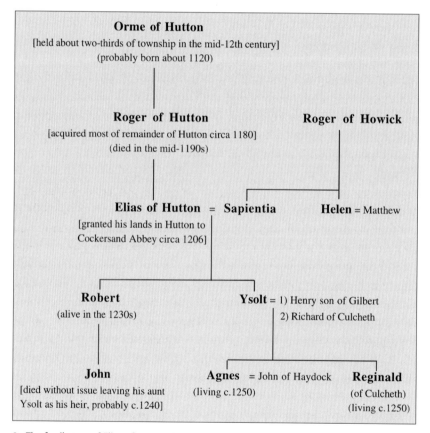

Orme of Hutton
[held about two-thirds of township in the mid-12th century]
(probably born about 1120)

Roger of Hutton
[acquired most of remainder of Hutton circa 1180]
(died in the mid-1190s)

Roger of Howick

Elias of Hutton = **Sapientia**
[granted his lands in Hutton to Cockersand Abbey circa 1206]

Helen = Matthew

Robert
(alive in the 1230s)

Ysolt = 1) Henry son of Gilbert
2) Richard of Culcheth

John
[died without issue leaving his aunt Ysolt as his heir, probably c.1240]

Agnes = John of Haydock
(living c.1250)

Reginald
(of Culcheth)
(living c.1250)

2. The family tree of Elias of Hutton, benefactor of Cockersand Abbey: this tree is based on the evidence provided by the charters and other documents preserved among the archives of the abbey. It is not possible to give precise dates for the lives of these people but the relationships shown are accurate. This is the first Hutton family of whom we have any detailed information – it is comparatively unusual to have even an outline family tree for an ordinary family eight hundred years ago.

not efficient to administer or to farm, and many landowners negotiated with each other to exchange or sell fragmented properties and so to consolidate their holdings into one area. Roger, son of Orme, inherited his father's property at Heaton and in the late 1170s or early 1180s he made a 'swapping arrangement' with Roger, son of Ranulf of Marsey, and Augustine, son of Waldeve of Ulverston. By this agreement, the Heaton (Lancaster) estate was transferred to Augustine, and Roger, son of Orme, in exchange took possession of the estate in Hutton which Augustine had inherited from his father, Waldeve. This made much more sense: Roger, son of Orme, now held almost the whole of Hutton, while Augustine added the Heaton property to his existing estates around Morecambe Bay.[7] None of these men had outright ownership of the lands in question, for all of them had overlords to whom they were chief tenants. In the case of the Hutton estates the ultimate lords were the de Lacy family, earls of Lincoln, whose vast territories in east Lancashire and the West Riding of Yorkshire were centred on their castles at Clitheroe and Pontefract. The feudal overlords of Hutton were originally the barons of Penwortham, from whom the township was held in exchange for dues of military service, but in 1204 the overlordship had passed to the de Laceys.

Roger, son of Orme, probably died in the 1190s and was succeeded as lord of Hutton by his son Elias, the benefactor of Cockersand. A series of deeds shows that by grants during the first half of the thirteenth century Elias and his wife Sapientia richly endowed the abbey, a policy continued in the next generation by their heirs. These documents not only tell us about Hutton, but also allow us to reconstruct the family tree of the donors, the first family in Hutton of whom we have any record. Elias and Sapientia had a son, Robert, and at least one daughter, who bore the romantic Arthurian name of Ysolt or Ysolde. Robert had children but his sister Ysolt eventually became the sole heiress of the estates (other than those already alienated, or transferred, to the ownership of Cockersand) which had been built up by her forebears. She was married twice, firstly to Henry, son of Gilbert, and secondly to Richard de Culcheth. All these people continued to favour Cockersand, so that for almost a century the family of Elias de Hutton were among the principal benefactors of the abbey.

The land which Elias gave totalled three *carucates*, a unit of land measurement which is often translated into modern English as a teamland or ploughland (in other words, the area of arable land which could be ploughed by a single team of horses or oxen). In reality, by the time these documents were being produced in the thirteenth century, the term had lost its precision and varied very widely from place to place. It may be sufficient, and more realistic, to say that the total area given by Elias and other members of his family was probably about 1200 acres, including substantial areas of mossland, common grazing land and marsh, and not to try to be more specific than that. Although Elias was the landowner, the feudal overlord was Robert de Lacey, from whom he held the land for the feudal due of one-fourth of a knight's fee.[8] In 1232 x 1240[9] John de Lacey, earl of Lincoln, gave his formal approval (as lord of Hutton) to the earlier transfer of ownership to Cockersand, and in about 1290 John's grandson, Henry de Lacey, confirmed it once more. The monasteries often insisted upon the issuing of such confirmations to make their legal title to the estates perfectly clear.

The original gift of land by Elias was made no later than Easter 1210, and probably significantly earlier than that. In the twelfth and early thirteenth centuries precise dating of documents in the modern fashion was rare, and we do not know exactly when the transaction was made, but on 30 March 1210 a verdict was made in the name of Pope Innocent III concerning a dispute between Cockersand Abbey and Evesham Abbey (the mother house of the recently-founded small priory at Penwortham) over the Hutton estates. This dispute is considered in more detail below, but the document confirms that by then Cockersand owned its Hutton estate. Since there must have been time for a dispute to arise and go to arbitration, we may suppose that they had owned the land for at least three or four years, pushing the date back to 1206 or earlier.

We also know that the land eventually granted to Cockersand had previously been rented by them from Elias. A deed whereby Elias leased property to Alice, daughter of Ketel, and her two sons Richard and Robert, refers to the land which the canons of Cockersand held from him as tenants. The deed was witnessed by Henry of Ribbleton, who died at Eastertide 1201, so we know that in the late 1190s the abbey was already occupying the property. As the abbey was not itself founded until about 1190, this was therefore one of its earliest territorial acquisitions. We therefore have good grounds for supposing that Cockersand took a lease on the estate at Hutton in the mid-1190s and then in about 1205 was granted that property outright by its owner, Elias.[10] A subsequent entry in the cartulary tells us that this grant was further reiterated and confirmed by Elias sometime between 1210 and 1220, at which time it was stated (not quite correctly) that the estate covered 'the whole of the town of Hutton in Leylandshire'.[11] The grant by Elias was repeated by his son, Robert, who in 1220×1246 issued a quitclaim (as its name suggests, a formal renunciation of all rights) to the property. In the same period his sister, Ysolt, daughter of Elias, 'in her widowhood' granted Cockersand 'all the land which her father gave to her in marriage' – that is, her dowry on marriage to Henry de Culcheth had included land in Hutton. Finally, in 1240×1256, there was a grand recitation of the legal title, in which the former owners renounced all and every possible claim. John of Haydock and his wife Agnes (who was the daughter of Ysolt) granted to Cockersand 'the land in Hutton which belonged to them by reason of their marriage and which is called Ysolt's land', reciting the charter whereby Ysolt in her widowhood had granted the land to her daughter and son-in-law. The renunciation also included a cancellation of the charter whereby Richard of Culcheth, Agnes' father and Ysolt's husband, had granted land to his daughter on marriage; the charter which Reginald of Culcheth, Alice's brother, had issued for John of Haydock; the charter of Elias, son of Roger, granting lands to Henry, son of Gilbert, the first husband of Ysolt; and, finally, the quitclaim made by Richard de Culcheth to the land called Ysolt's land. This comprehensive set of legal documents established, as far as possible at a time when many legal processes were still relatively unsophisticated, that Cockersand definitely owned the Hutton estates.[12]

Although the family of Elias of Hutton were the main landowners in the late twelfth and early thirteenth centuries, there were others. Numerous documents survive from the century after 1200 to illustrate the way in which Cockersand and, to a much lesser extent, Evesham abbeys became the dominant landowners in the township. As well as those recited in the Cockersand cartulary there are significant collections of early medieval deeds in the Farington of Worden and Hesketh of Rufford collections at the Lancashire Record Office, both of these families eventually acquiring estates in Hutton. It is rarely possible to pinpoint the exact location of the properties in question. There is little evidence of the field names or, if names are given, they have long since fallen out of use and their whereabouts are now more or less unknown. Among the minor land-owners were the co-heirs of Robert, son of Bernard de Goosnargh, and

Geoffrey de Longton and his son Robert. These people are recorded because eventually they too gave endowments to Cockersand. However, much more complicated was the small estate held by the parish church of St Mary in Penwortham. It was quite common in the early Middle Ages for individuals to give lands to parish churches, just as others did to monastic houses. The rents from the land were intended to provide funds for the upkeep of the fabric, the saying of masses for the souls of the benefactor, and other pious uses. But Penwortham church was itself one of the endowments of the Benedictine priory of Penwortham, a minor and subordinate daughter-house of Evesham, one of the wealthiest and most influential of all English monasteries. Hutton was entirely within the parish of Penwortham and the tithes [13] of Hutton were therefore payable to Penwortham church and hence to Evesham. Thus, according to one interpretation of an extremely ambiguous law, Cockersand, as owner of the Hutton estates, should have paid a tithe of produce to Evesham. This would not only have been expensive but also humiliating, for no monastic house would wish to be beholden to another – especially one of a different religious order. Cockersand therefore refused to pay the tithes and Evesham took the matter through the church courts.

On 30 March 1210 it was decided by assessors that Cockersand should be exempted from the payment of tithes to Evesham, but that the latter – which clearly had legal right on its side – should receive in compensation the sum of 30 shillings a year. This agreement was finally sealed in 1215, and thereafter Penwortham church and priory only received the tithes on the land which it held directly: a deed of the 1230s, for example, refers to the grant of lands in the area west of Liverpool Road, 'excluding from Marshall's furlong eighteen acres of land on the eastern side, the tithes of which the church of Penwortham collects'.[14] However, tensions between the two monasteries continued and the dispute flared up in 1237 and again in 1273. In that year the monks of Evesham claimed, despite the decision of 1210, that the tithes of Hutton had been illegally alienated ('given away') by their predecessors, and that since then they had increased in annual value by at least ten shillings. Cockersand argued that, firstly, the 1210–1215 decision had been entirely lawful; secondly, the increase in value had been nothing like ten shillings; and thirdly, that any increase had been entirely the result of labours by the monks, so that morally this growth in value was irrelevant. A hearing at Warwick determined that the exemption should continue but that the compensatory payment should be increased to 34 shillings a year.[15]

4. The Landscape of Medieval Hutton

The many early medieval deeds help us to reconstruct, albeit very tentatively, the landscape of the township. We cannot produce a definitive map but the descriptions of boundaries and locations does provide a picture of the land use and major landmarks of the time. Perhaps the most important is that deed whereby Ysolt, daughter of Elias, gave the land which she had from her father. It can be loosely rendered in modern English as 'from the chapel of Uvedale going up towards the croft of Elias, as far as the dyke which is between that croft and Buresgreave, then along that dyke as far as the middle of the carr[16] which is the division between Hutton and Howick, along that carr up as far as the clough towards the Cockersand land, along that clough up as far as the way out of the out-lane, then along the out-lane as far as the dyke on the western side, and along the dyke in a straight line as far as another out-lane, and along that out-lane into Uvedale again, to the chapel'. An earlier grant, made by Elias himself, gives to Cockersand the property formerly held by Richard Scathe, including a toft and croft (a small-holding and garden) and an orchard, together with the lands held by Ysolt, and 'the Croke lands next to the road from the town, and the land between the land of Hugh Ronel and Jordan del Mor in length from the marsh to the headland, and the land of *Lairsclade* unto Calf (a ditch or small stream), as Calf runs down into the Great Pool, and as the Pool goes up towards Lairsclade, and the land lying between the land of Saint Mary of Penwortham unto the land of Richard Scathe, upon the Great Marsh in width, and in length by the sand to the pool'. A third grant, by Robert, son of Elias, confirms his father's gifts and adds to that estate another property, 'from the vivary [fishing ponds] within Harecarr two perches unto the division of Howick, going up that division southward unto Buresgreave, along the same unto Uvesdale, unto the chapel ditch, along the ditch unto the vivary again'.[17]

Nothing is known of the chapel mentioned in several of these

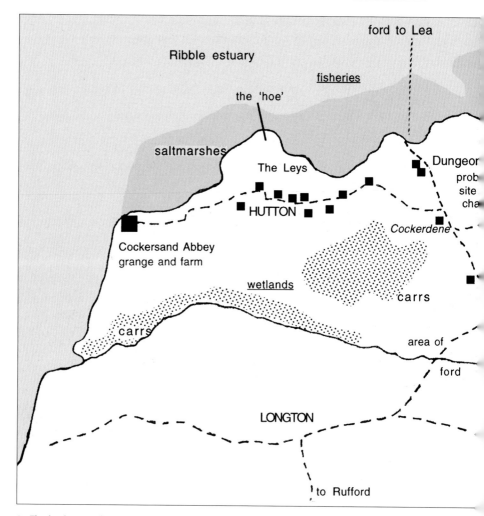

3. The landscape of medieval Hutton: a tentative reconstruction based on the evidence of the Cockersand cartulary. Note the five distinct bands of different land uses, with (west to east) the estuarine salt marshes; the 'settled' farmland interspersed with patches of wetland (carrs); the open arable fields; the grazing moor; and the moss or wetland at the eastern extremity of the township.

documents but their dating confirms that it was in existence by the late twelfth century and probably a good deal earlier. Traditionally it was said to have been on the edge of the old shore just north-east of Dungeon Farm, where the name Chapel Hill is marked on older maps. If this is so, and modern research suggests that this location is plausible, all trace of it has long since vanished and no archaeological investigation has

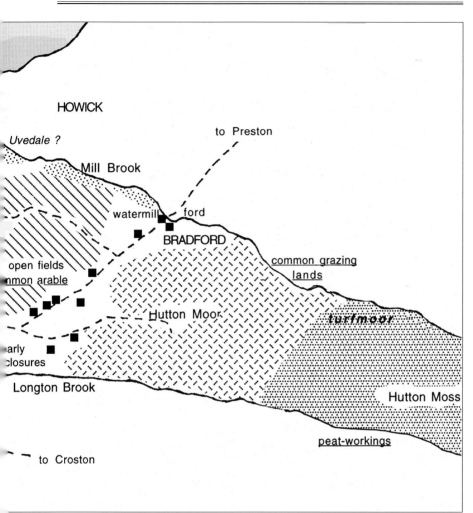

been undertaken. The location is clearly very significant, for the low hill on which the chapel stood is just above the lane (now marked in part by Skip Lane) which led down to the crossing over the Ribble sands to Lea. There was unquestionably such a crossing or ford in the Middle Ages and it was sufficiently well used for a guide stationed permanently on the Lea side to assist travellers. It is therefore likely that the chapel at Hutton was for the benefit of those crossing the river and using what was probably an important north-south routeway from the Fylde into south-west Lancashire. Among those using the ford would have been monastic officials travelling between Cockersand and its south Lancashire estates, including Hutton itself. Chapels by the wayside or at major river crossings are well-attested from the medieval period, and this seems a convincing context for the chapel at Hutton.

The abbey was given almost the whole of Hutton and had extensive properties in other parts of Lancashire. Their main value to the monastery was that these lands generated a large income from rents, so Cockersand, like almost all religious houses, leased out most of its new estates to tenants. Some of the leases are also recorded in the cartulary, giving further information about boundaries and the landscape. Thus, in 1216 x 1235 Cockersand leased an area of farmland to Alexander, son of Richard Scathe, and the deed recited its boundaries in great detail: 'from the dyke along the land of Roger Breton to the south, as far as Middle-syke, then following Middlesyke to the old ditch to the north then to Leirburnsike, then to the first dyke, then following this dyke to the north as far as Opwarphdelondes coming from Kokerdene, then following the dyke to the bounds of the town, then to the lands of Roger Breton; also part of our land near the sike (a small stream or ditch) of Bradford, following the sike to the moss, following the moss to the sike, and descending to the south by the sike to the Great Leach, following the Great Leach to the Maingate at the east end of the ditch of Henry of Culcheth, then following the sike to Bradford, and one acre in Kokerdene'.[18] These verbal descriptions, so characteristic of deeds in this period (for drawing maps to illustrate locations and boundaries would not become commonplace until the seventeenth century), speak of places familiar and readily comprehensible to contemporaries, but ambiguous to us unless we have other evidence with which to cross-reference. By and large, unfortunately, we do not have that evidence, but we can draw useful conclusions from some of the details given and we can deduce much about the landscape of medieval Hutton.

At the western end of the township was the saltmarsh, which was used for grazing land when uncovered by the tide. Along the Ribble estuary from Crossens round to Lytham the marsh was exploited in this way, its short wiry turf and very high natural salt content being held to give a particularly fine flavour to the animals grazed there. A more immediate benefit was that the unreclaimed marsh was manorial waste and could be considered as a communal resource which did not have alternative uses – it was, therefore, a valuable addition to the onshore pastures. The marsh extended outwards from the foot of the steep slopes which marked the old shoreline, and over the centuries the inner sections of marsh, furthest from open water, were gradually reclaimed and converted to improved pasture. This process is well-documented along the north Lancashire coast and took place in Hutton from at least the

4. The steep slope from Grange Lane and Bottom of Hutton down to the flat fields alongside the river marks the ancient shoreline of the Ribble estuary. Eight centuries ago most of the land shown in this view would have been under water.

fifteenth century. It is specifically described in the Rawstorne estate records of the early eighteenth century. On the sands and the marshes of Hutton there were fisheries. One of the earliest deeds, by which Elias gave to Cockersand the lands formerly tenanted by Richard Scathe, also granted to the monks the right to have 'three nets to be freely fixed in Ribble water anywhere within the bounds of Hutton'. Robert, son of Elias, in confirming these grants, referred to 'the whole fishery in Ribble belonging to the town of Hutton', while in 1200×1236 Abel of Hutton quitclaimed to Cockersand 'three stakenets in Ribble, within the bounds of Hutton'.[19] An unusually detailed reference occurs in 1200×1230 when, in consideration of the large sum of 10 shillings in silver, Adam, son of Geoffrey de Longton, gave the canons of Cockersand the site of a trammel net 'in the best place within the bounds of Hutton' which had been granted to him by Elias. A trammel net was one with a double layer, a fine inner mesh which the fish pushed between the holes of a coarse outer net, so that they trapped themselves in a sort of pocket. In 1268×1279 Richard, son of Robert the Scrivener (scribe) held from Cockersand the right to place nets, including four stake-nets, in the Ribble from the boundary of Howick to the boundary of Clifton, confirming that the fisheries of Hutton extended out to the township boundary which followed the main channel in the middle of the estuary. Freshwater fish were also taken: as noted above, there was a *vivary* or fishpond within the wetland area known as Harecarr, close to the Howick boundary north of Ratten Row, which is mentioned in several deeds of 1220×1246.[20]

5. *Hutton Moss*

At the opposite end of the township was the moss, the expanse of peat bog which extended into the adjacent wetlands of Penwortham, Farington and Longton and was almost at the northernmost end of a great tract of such land reaching down into south-west Lancashire. The moss was important as a source of rushes and reeds for thatching, and for use in candles and tallow lights (the pith from reeds was dried and used as the wick), of waterfowl and fish, and of brushwood and willows for

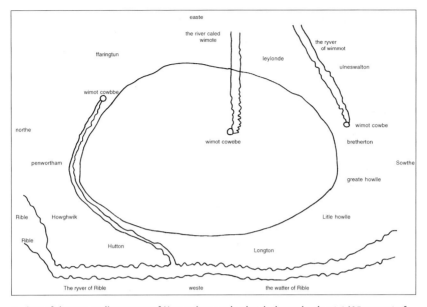

easte

the river caled wimote

ffaringtun

the ryver of wimmot

leylonde

ulneswalton

wimot cowbbe

northe

wimot cowebe

wimot cowbe

bretherton

penwortham

Sowthe

greate howlle

Rible Howghwik

Litle howlle

Rible

Hutton Longton

The ryver of Rible weste the watter of Rible

5. One of the two earliest maps of Hutton is a crude sketch drawn in about 1605 as part of the evidence presented during litigation over turbary (peat-digging) rights on the local mosses. This redrawn version shows the main landmarks of interest to the arbitrators. In the centre is a large oval which represents the unenclosed mossland belonging to Hutton, Farington, Leyland, Ulnes Walton and Longton, in the vicinity of what is now Whitestake and New Longton. The neighbouring townships are named and three streams, each called Wymot, are shown flowing off the moss. (Based on LRO DDF 543.)

baskets and other household items. Most crucially though, the moss was essential because until the late eighteenth century its turf or peat was the only readily-available domestic fuel, and all over the Lancashire plain the mosses were exploited as turbaries (from the medieval Latin *turbarium*, a peat-working). We have only a few contemporary references to peat-diggings on Hutton Moss, although in nearby Penwortham they are well-documented. The only early medieval Hutton record is the place-name 'Turfmoor-furlong', mentioned in a deed of 1212 x 1246 and situated close to the Howick boundary east of Liverpool Road, but the existence of the name at this early date implies that the peat-workings were already well-established in the late twelfth century. There are also a couple of late medieval references: in September 1518, for example, William Bic-kerstath leased from John Strickland and Richard Hesketh 'all that turbary in Hutton next to Whymott called the Turfroom'.[21] while the accounts prepared in 1538–1539 on the dissolution of Cockersand abbey, based on the last full year's rental, refer to the leasing to Thomas Tipping and William Bostock for twopence a year of turbary or 'mosse rowmez' on Hutton Moss. A moss-room or turf-room was an area of moss allocated to an individual or institution, and both these references show that the term was in everyday use here as it was in neighbouring townships.[22]

The moss is one of the main features shown on the earliest surviving map of Hutton, a rough plan made in about 1605 to show landmarks and other essential information concerned with a legal dispute over enclosures and peat-workings. There were several long-running court cases over the ownership and management of mosslands in the area during the later sixteenth and early seventeenth centuries – others related to Penwortham, Walton-le-Dale and Farington – and the arbitrators in these cases needed plans to help them to understand the intricacies of arguments about local geography. The 1605 map is accompanied by a second plan, which is no more than a crude sketch, and by detailed notes or annotations which help to explain the case. These indicate that the documents were produced for, or possibly written personally by, William Farington of Worden in Leyland, who is known to have been engaged in several turbary disputes in this period, and among whose papers these items survived.[23]

The memoranda include a series of statements about *moss doles*, which were the allocations of sections of the moss for peat-working. Thus, it is stated that there was 'a dowell of mosse being upon the west syde of the waye that leadeth from mylners platte unto the [division] of the mosse betwixt longton and hutton is iiij rodes[24] & a halfe in bredth after the rate of viij yardes to the rode'. This was followed, moving eastwards, by another allotment of moss belonging to Robert Hesketh, which had been bought from the grandfather of Lewis Longton; a dole belonging to Richard Fleetwood of Penwortham; a dole 'of mye inherytance' (that is, belonging to Farington); a dole held by Lewis Longton; a small dole, only three rods wide, owned by Rawstorne; another dole held by Lewis Longton; and one which was described in more detail: 'a parcell of mosse lande now the inherytanse of the sayd Richard Fletewodde & late the inherytanse of the awnsestowre (ancestor) of the said Lewase Longton occupied by the late pryor of Penwortham'. Finally, it says, all the land east from this dole belongs to Mr Rawstorne, the lord of the manor. Another note gives the length of some of these allocations of moss land. The first mentioned is 76 rods long, and the dole owned by Farington was 33 rods in length – a rod was a measure which in this area was probably eight yards (roughly two metres).

From this we can reconstruct at least something of how the moss was divided. The dimensions are in Lancashire measure, which was considerably larger than statute measure, but if put in the latter form the moss allocation (dole, or room) first mentioned as 4½ rods by 76 rods would be about 600 yards by 36 yards, or 4½ acres, while the smaller one owned by Farington was roughly 264 yards by 24 yards and so came to 1⅓ acres. The area described lay south of Nutters Platt and along Green Lane. According to a note on the 1605 map, the total area of moss in Hutton had been calculated in 1602 by a Mr Moor, who arrived at a figure of about 280 acres in modern statute measure, though this is significantly less than its earlier extent since reclamation had already taken place. The descriptions also confirm that in Hutton, as in other townships in the area, portions of the turbary rights within the moss had been sold off or leased to different landowners during the Middle Ages. Although the Rawstornes (lords of the manor after 1546) retained ultimate rights over the waste, the Faringtons and the Fleetwoods, as well as a couple of lesser owners, had secured effective control of areas of turbary. It is of particular interest that the priory of Penwortham had had an allocation of mossland, presumably by virtue of its possession of an estate within the township. Although in national terms a small and insignificant religious house, the priory was a local landowner of some importance and was active in exploiting the peat resources of the mosses in the vicinity.

Although the moss was the largest area of wetland in the township, there were other smaller patches, some of which survive even today despite large-scale drainage works over the centuries. In Lancashire such boggy patches were called 'carrs' (from the Norse *kjarr*, an area of overgrown or brush-covered bog or swamp). Many of the early medieval deeds refer to carrs, but on these wet tracts within the farmed area some drainage work was already under way by the beginning of the thirteenth century, possibly in response to the rapid growth in population which is attested throughout the country in this period. With more mouths to feed, additional land had to be brought into cultivation and existing agricultural land improved so that it produced larger yields. In lowland Lancashire drainage was an important way of achieving this goal. Ditches

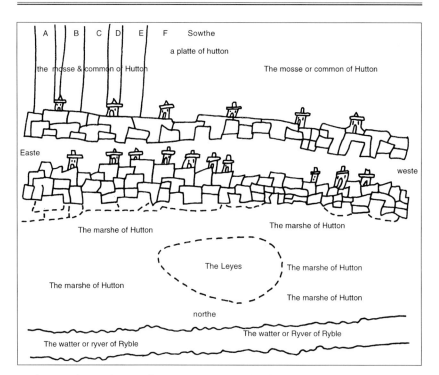

A B C D E F   Sowthe

a platte of hutton

the mosse & common of Hutton   The mosse or common of Hutton

Easte

weste

The marshe of Hutton   The marshe of Hutton

The Leyes   The marshe of Hutton

The marshe of Hutton

The marshe of Hutton   The marshe of Hutton

northe

The watter or Ryver of Ryble

The watter or ryver of Ryble

6. The second map of Hutton drawn in 1605 is more detailed. It shows the Ribble at the bottom (north) with the grazing lands of The Leys almost surrounded by the Hutton marshes. South of these, towards the top of the map, are two belts of farmed land. The more northerly is the old agricultural lands in the Grange Lane and Liverpool Road area, while the southerly (nearer the top) is the newer enclosed lands along Moor Lane. At the top are the mosses of Hutton. The map shows several long narrow divisions which represent the allotments of turbary (peat-digging) rights into which the moss was divided. The original map is annotated with details of these allocations – the key to this redrawn version is given below.

A this is a parcell of Mr Fletewoddes parcells of the mosse
B one of the dowelles of the mosse claymed by Mr ffarington & Mr Rawstorne
C Mr Rawstorne hath a dowelle of mosse here lying
D Mr Fletewoddes dowel of mosse purchased of Mr Longton
E the seconde dowelle of mosse claymed by Mr ffarington which he purchased of Mr Longton
F Mr Rawstornes mosse dowelles with others

were dug to carry away the surplus water, and the boggy streams were straightened and deepened to increase capacity and run-off. As the ground dried out it could become improved pasture or might even be adaptable for arable cultivation. The smaller carrs in the west of the township were tackled at an early stage. When Cockersand leased land near Cockerton to Alexander Scathe in about 1225 one of the boundary marks mentioned was 'the old ditch', which implies that drainage work had been undertaken in that area many years before – perhaps in the middle years of the twelfth century but conceivably even earlier than that.[25] The phrase is echoed by the name 'old rean' (ditch) which is given in a deed of 1216 x 1250, referring to a channel or watercourse which ran from the vicinity of Tithebarn Farm towards the Longton boundary. Many documents from this period refers to stretches of 'dike' or ditches, such as the Chapel Ditch, south of Chapel Hill and east of Dungeon.[26] The impression is that even as early as the late twelfth century there was a substantial network of drainage ditches and man-made watercourses, supplementing and improving the natural channels flowing westwards from the moss.

There were more continuous stretches of wetland along the shallow valley of the Mill Brook, then known as Uvedale. A grant of land to Cockersand by Ysolt, daughter of Elias, describes the boundary as going 'along that dyke ... unto the midst of the carr which is the division between Hutton and Howick', while in the 1220s Roger, son of Geoffrey de Longton, made a quitclaim in favour of Cockersand of 'pasture for sixteen oxen upon the carr of Howick', the boundary of which ran 'between the marsh and the hard land of Howick-carr',[27] an area on the Howick border at the lower end of the Mill Brook valley. The same document refers revealingly to 'the new dyke', indicating that reclamation work was already actively in progress in the area even in the early years of the Cockersand lordship.[28] Such work continued, for in September 1272 Henry de Lacey, earl of Lincoln and overlord of Hutton, gave Cockersand the right to 'raise a dyke upon their own lands through the midst of Hoham-carr, beginning at Mark-pool and extending to Land-mere-pool', while at some point in the 1240s Adam, son of Mary de Howick, had issued a quitclaim of land in Hutton 'from the half of Risebriche across the Carr' towards the Ribble. A 'rising-bridge' (*hrisen-brig*) was a brushwood causeway laid across wet and marshy ground.[29] Despite all this activity considerable areas of open carr remained into the later medieval period: in 1451, for example, the rental of Cockersand abbey notes that for the use of the carr next to Bradford Greaves, the tenants in Hutton paid a collective rent of twelve hens,[30] while in the eighteenth century the surviving areas of carr were adapted for use as osier beds, supplying a craft which gained some importance locally – osiers were a variety of willow, used in basket-making.

6. The Moor and the Open Fields

Hutton Moor, an area of open grazing land, lay between Liverpool Road and the edge of the moss. The edge of the moor was a desirable area for settlement, because it was comparatively dry and had good access to several different types of land – the grasslands of the moor itself, the wetlands and peat workings of the moss, the arable fields west of the main road, and, without much difficulty, the marshes at the bottom of the slope. It is perhaps significant that, as surnames began to develop in the fourteenth century, a number of local people took theirs from the fact that they lived by the moor: thus, in 1347 Patrick del' More of Hutton is recorded.[31] The moor, being comparatively well-drained, was also an obvious area for enclosure and the creation of improved pasture, and this ultimately led to its disappearance. We know from place-name and other evidence that it must originally have extended from Liverpool Road almost as far as Nutters Platt and Workhouse Lane (Pope Lane), but by the sixteenth century it had been substantially reduced in extent. The earliest enclosures [32] were in the vicinity of Moor Lane, where they added to existing farmland, but then the process of enclosure gradually moved south-eastwards into the interior of the moor, eventually allowing the creation of several new farms on the former grazing land. Although in the early Middle Ages the moor probably covered about 500 acres, by the time Mr Moor surveyed and measured the township in 1602 this had shrunk to only 150 acres. There was one other area of communal grazing land, known as The Leys, situated immediately north of Bottom of Hutton just in from the edge of the saltmarsh. This land was communally managed as a grazing moor under manorial control, the tenants paying a nominal collective rent for the privilege of turning their animals onto the land. It, too, was reduced in size by enclosure. In the 1451 Cockersand rental it is stated that *omnis tenens de Hotton dat' domino pro Leyse juxta Rybyll 48 gall'* (all the tenants of Hutton render to the lord for the Leys next to the Ribble, 48 hens), which suggests that it was a reasonably substantial area of land. By 1602, however, 'the lyes' covered only 13½ statute acres in total.[33]

In the early Middle Ages most of the arable land of Hutton, which

7. The fields opposite the Grammar School are part of the area which used to be the open grazing land of Hutton Moor. These tracts of rough grassland were fenced and enclosed in the sixteenth century and by 1780 all the moor had been divided between private owners.

lay entirely on the relatively narrow belt of drier land in the centre of the township, was arranged in open fields in which individual tenants of Cockersand, together with freeholders and tenants of the other minor lords, were allocated strips. These strips within the open field were technically known as *selions*. a term used in several deeds of the thirteenth and fourteenth centuries. Thus, in November 1332 Matilda, daughter of Adam del' More of Hutton, granted to Thomas de Marton a house and two selions of land in Hutton, adjacent to the lands of the abbot of Cockersand, while ten years later 'Adam son of William son of Hugh of Hutton' granted to Robert de Blackburn a total of ten selions between the lands of Robert de Ainsdale on the east and Greengate on the west, and in Moorflat near the lands of the abbot and of Henry de Mawdesley.[34] We do not know how many open fields there were, but it is certain that they were irregular in shape and did not resemble the classic system which operated in the English Midlands, whereby there were three large

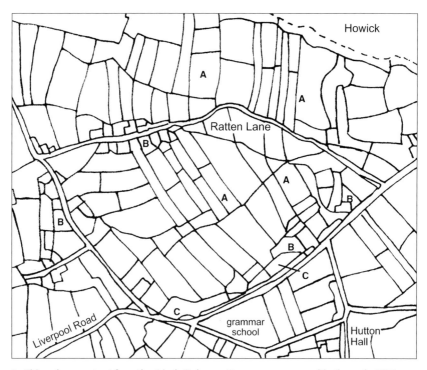

8. This redrawn extract from the 6-inch Ordnance Survey map surveyed in the early 1840s shows the pattern of fields and enclosures in the area centred on Hutton Row and the *Anchor Inn*. This was the heart of the community by the 1840s, although in the Middle Ages the main focus had been further to the north-west, along Grange Lane and around Bottom of Hutton. Even in the 1840s the medieval field pattern was clear. The many long narrow strip-shaped fields (A) on both sides of Ratten Lane (then called Nook Lane), northwards towards the Mill Brook and southwards towards Liverpool Road, were the enclosed remnants of the medieval open arable strips. They contrast with the jumble of tiny enclosed plots along Liverpool Road (B), at Ratten Row and on Skip Lane, which represent piecemeal enclosure from the former common waste. Many of these plots were occupied by the small cottages of agricultural labourers. In some places, as at (C), it is apparent that long strips of roadside verge have been fenced off to make elongated fields, which later became useful building land and led to ribbon-type development in the vicinity of Hutton village.

fields of which at any time one was left fallow. That was not the Lancashire practice and, given the broken topography and small size of Hutton, a much less formal and more fragmented pattern is very probable. The most important field lay west of Liverpool Road, north of Hutton Row and the Anchor. Here a pattern of long narrow fields was still evident in the mid-nineteenth century and these represented the 'fossilised' strips of the former open field, which was known as Hutton Field or Town Field. Parcels of land in this area were referred to in, for example, a lease for twenty years made in January 1461 by John Holland of Hutton to Richard Sherdley, whereby all properties held by John were leased 'except two acres next to Hutton Field'; a deed of the 1570s which mentions 'land in Hutton Town Feild adjoining at the east to Ditch Greave Balk'; and one of February 1621 by which 'a close or parcel of land in the town field called Sower Buttes' was rented out. There were certainly other fields, but they may well have been very small and they probably did not survive into the seventeenth century. Although the open fields of Hutton are thus rather poorly-documented, and have left relatively little trace, it is instructive to note that at neighbouring Longton the pattern of long narrow fields survived in a remarkably complete fashion into the late nineteenth century, and is splendidly mapped on the 1st edition 6-inch Ordnance Survey map of the 1840s. Even today in Longton there are, despite the major changes in agriculture and the extensive building development of the twentieth century, many traces of this field pattern.[35]

The general trend, from at least the thirteenth century, was towards the enclosure of open land and common land, to create hedged or fenced fields restricted to the private use of the landowner or tenant. Sometimes documents refer obliquely to this process. A deed of October 1529, for example, relates to one acre of arable land in Hutton called Papes Hill Acre, the phrasing and name of which make it clear that this was an enclosed field. Very much earlier there is evidence of the fragmentation of land holdings and the creation of tiny parcels of land which is probably associated with the trend towards enclosure. Thus, when in 1200 x 1236 Abel de Hutton made various grants to Cockersand the documents refer to two parcels of land of unstated area; one parcel of just over three acres; one 'land' of half an acre; two 'lands' of a quarter of an acre each; and other small pieces, which were subdivided among five sub-tenants in return for small rents. The impression is that in parts of Hutton (these examples lay close to the main road) the landholdings were being divided and re-divided to make smallholdings and crofts, a process which we can link to the rapid population growth in the thirteenth century. There was pressure on the land, more mouths to feed, and more families to be accommodated somehow. Subdivision and fragmentation were the probable response.[36]

In contrast to this pattern of subdivision, the manorial lord of Hutton, Cockersand Abbey, retained one very large estate for its own use. This

The rental of Cockersand Abbey tenants in Hutton in 1451

A rental was a list of those who paid rent to a landlord, and often included details of what each tenant held as well as the rent which he or she paid. Below is given an adapted version of the 1451 rental of the properties in Hutton which were owned by Cockersand Abbey. It was almost certainly compiled by the abbey's steward. The amounts involved did not normally vary from year to year, so that he may simply have copied out the wording of rentals from previous years. Note that by this date all the monastic lands in Hutton were rented out, rather than being held directly by the abbey – even the lordship of the manor of Hutton was sub-let, as the first line indicates.

	Name of tenant and property held	*Annual rent payable*		
1451	Ralph Blackburn, manor of Hutton with appurtenances	£12	6s.	8d.
	Thomas Milner, 1 tenement* with Bradforth Grevys		32s.	
	Wilcott Milner, 1 tenement		17s.	
	Thomas Milner, a watermill with 1 close		26s.	8d.
	Thomas Atkinson, 1 tenement		9s.	
	Richard Baxter, 1 tenement		13s.	4d.
	Robert Wilding, 1 tenement		26s.	8d.
	John Mayre, 1 tenement		20s.	
	Lewis Cutler, 1 tenement		14s.	8d.
	John Mayre, 1 tenement		16s.	
	Thomas Wilding, 1 tenement		18s.	
	Hugh Jenkinson, 1 tenement		17s.	
	Thomas Eaves, 1 tenement		15s.	10d.
	Richard Glave, 1 tenement		22s.	
	Ralph Hodgeson, 1 tenement		22s.	9d.
	Thomas Kirkby, 6 acres		7s.	
	Thomas Garstang, 1 toft†			8d.

omnis tenens de Hotton dat domino pro les Leyse juxta Ribyll
[all the tenants of Hutton give for [the use of grazing in] The
    Leas next to the Ribble]   48 cocks

ibidem tenentes pro del Carr' juxta Bradforth Grevys
[the like tenants for [the use of] the carr next to Bradford Greaves] 12 cocks

(adapted from Cockersand Cartulary, pp.1254–55)

* *tenement* means a landholding, normally with a dwelling; it does not imply
    the more recent sense of the word as in, e.g., a Glasgow tenement.
† a *toft* is a small enclosed area or backland, equivalent to the modern idea
    of a small garden or allotment.

was the demesne farm at Hutton Grange, the name of which provides a direct link with the medieval past. The term 'grange' is found very frequently on former monastic properties and, except where used in recent times in a consciously antiquarian way to mean a large house, it invariably identifies a substantial commercial farm of the early medieval period. In the twelfth and thirteenth centuries most larger monasteries established granges on their outlying properties, staffed with lay brethren and hired labourers and exploited directly for the benefit of the religious house produce was sent back to supply the monastic kitchens, or was sold on local markets to provide a cash revenue. This is how Hutton Grange operated in its early years. It was almost certainly developed from an older property, probably the original manor house and home farm of Hutton, and was taken over by the monks when Elias granted the estate at the beginning of the thirteenth century. The first specific reference to the grange is in 1216×1250, when the road from the town to the grange is mentioned as a boundary.[37] The grange stood on the best land in the township, amid well-drained tracts of good or improvable pasture, with arable land close by, and the excellent grazing of the saltmarsh just below the property. It was close to what was then open water, so that some contacts between Hutton and Cockersand were almost certainly by coastal vessel rather than the route across the Ribble ford and then overland through the Fylde.

For perhaps a hundred years a large farming operation was managed by the monks and lay brethren who sent produce by road or boat up to Cockersand, or sold it on Preston market, the hard work being done by the lay brethren and local hired labourers who worked in the fields and pastures. Relatively quickly, though, monastic houses all over the country rethought their management strategies. The policy of farming the grange estates directly gave way to a more convenient alternative, whereby farms were let out to a tenant in return for a sizeable guaranteed rent income. The brethren were no longer directly involved, either as labourers or as the employers of labour. Instead, the the long-term leasing of a grange offered an attractive opportunity for lucrative investment by a secular tenant, who kept the profits from the grange, while the monastery – spared any of the burdens or problems of land management – gained a secure and reliable income. We do not know when this change occurred at Hutton, but it was probably no later than the mid-fourteenth century when, because of the immense economic disruption occasioned by the Black Death (1348–1351), many granges were leased out. It had definitely happened by 1451, when the abbey rental states that Ralph Blackburn held the manor of Hutton with appurtenances as tenant, for an annual rent of £12 6s. 8d. (£12.33). The same man was still tenant in 1461, but by 1501 the tenancy had passed to the Farington family of Worden. In that year Charles Farington held it for £12 a year, and his son Richard was tenant in 1537, when the rental entry refers to 'the manor of Hutton called Hutton Grange'.[38]

7. Medieval Roads and Tracks

The roads and tracks of Hutton are little documented in the medieval period, but many deeds and other documents make incidental references to them as a way of locating the position of property. We can be sure that there was a well-developed network of routes, but much interest attaches to the question of their character. A grant by the abbot of Cockersand to Alexander Scathe around 1225 [39] refers to the 'main gate' in the context of Hutton Moss, at the eastern end of the township, and this is clearly a *meanygate*, a term used even today for a track or lane which led out onto the moss. In earlier centuries it meant a semi-public road giving communal access to the moss for driving herds or flocks and (most importantly) to allow turf carts and sleds to be taken to and from the turbaries. In a deed of July 1342 there is reference to 'the Greengate',[40] a name for a lane or track which ran through the fields (in this case in the vicinity of Liverpool Road). 'Gate' is from the Norse *gata*, a lane or track (as in Fishergate in Preston), and does not have its modern standard English meaning. Some deeds refer to 'out-lanes' as boundaries, these being the tracks which led from cultivated and settled farmland into the areas of the township in communal use as grazing land. They were thus equivalent to the meanygates, but were used for driving cattle onto the moor: the present Moor Lane originated as such an out-lane in the early medieval period. Out-lanes were not public rights of way but were the property of those whose lands abutted them: thus, in the first decade of the thirteenth century Hugh Bonel granted Cockersand 'a common share of his out-lane' which was in the vicinity of Bottom of Hutton.[41]

These deeds refer to back lanes or occupation tracks, but other documents show that more substantial roads were in existence even in the thirteenth century. The decision of March 1210, settling the tithe dispute between Cockersand and Evesham, names the 'high road' as one of the boundaries of the lands in question, referring to the old Liverpool road, while a grant made by Alexander Scathe in about 1240 refers to the same road as 'the high road from Longton'. Scathe later made a quitclaim in which the road is described as the 'waingate', a term which means 'cart-road' and so confirms that Liverpool road was already a major route for wheeled carts and wagons.[42] It was not the only such road, though. A grant made by Hugh Bonel to Cockersand in 1216×1250 relates to a parcel of land one of the bounds of which is 'the road from the town [of Hutton] to the grange', or Grange Lane. The terminology suggests that this was more than a trackway or back lane, and other documents relating to the same road specifically describe it as the 'waingate'.[43] These are some of the earliest references to the use of wheeled vehicles from any Lancashire source. It is often claimed that there were few wheeled vehicles in the county before the eighteenth century, but references such as these effectively refute that notion.

The Ribble crossings were approached by lanes which led down to the shore and, as we have seen, the riverside and its marshes were crucial to the economy of every township from Lytham to Ashton and from Penwortham to North Meols. In all these places, therefore, the ancient orientation of the community was along lanes which extended from the shore, across the drier slopes above the river, onto the grazing moors and then ultimately to the moss. Although each showed variation in detail, that general pattern was repeated along both sides of the estuary. It had its origins in the pre-Conquest period, was reinforced in the Middle Ages and survived until the nineteenth century. Today it is possible to trace the effect of this older pattern, in which the shore was far from being a dead end, on the plan and topography of towns and villages which in other ways have been drastically altered by the changes of the twentieth century. At Penwortham, for example, there was an ancient routeway from the church, past the *Fleece Inn*, and then along Cop Lane, while at Longton the old village stretched for more than a mile along what are now Marsh Lane–Liverpool Road–Chapel Lane. The reason why today's Liverpool Road, coming from Hutton, makes the awkward bend at the Chapel Lane junction and again bends sharply at the Marsh Lane junction is that historically it was the secondary route, and the main road ran in a straight line from east to west. The same applies at Hutton, where – as noted earlier – the alignment of Skip Lane and Moor Lane was the more important axis in the township, extending from the shore, through the arable area, up to the moor and eventually onto the moss. Here, the comparable 'double bend' at the

Skip Lane/Moor Lane junctions emphasises that Liverpool Road used to be the less important of these routes.

Nevertheless, it was clearly recognised in the thirteenth century as a prominent landscape feature and also as a main internal division within the township. The road, then a wide trackway edged by broad verges, separated the arable and settled areas of the township to the west from the moss and moor to the east, and it appears in numerous deeds. On the northern edge of Hutton the road crossed the Mill Brook, which then as now was the boundary with Howick, at Bradford, the broad ford, just beside Howick School. Today it is impossible to visualise the medieval landscape in this vicinity because of the wholesale changes to the road itself in the late 1930s, when the A59 was made into a dual carriageway and raised on a wide embankment with the stream culverted beneath. In the Middle Ages the brook carried a much greater volume of water flowing westwards from the mosslands and the ford was a substantial feature as its name suggests. The flow was sufficient to drive a sizeable watermill on the western (downstream) side and in wet weather the crossing may have presented a considerable obstacle to travellers.

Perhaps the most intriguing and potentially the most important reference to a road is in a deed of 1236 x 1246, whereby Robert, abbot of Evesham, leased a block of land to Robert le Sureis. The boundaries are described: 'from Cockerdene following the land of Roger Breton towards the east, to the bounds of the land of Cockersand and so on the east following the extremity of Ramkelcroft to the south as far as the *stratam ferratam* following which to Cockerdene'.[44] The term *stratam ferratam* means 'metalled road' and when used in early medieval documents is normally considered to relate to a former Roman road. Medieval roads were not metalled so the state of such routes was distinctive. While we cannot be certain which road is referred to, the implication is that it was Skip Lane, running south from the shore at Dungeon, past Cockerton Farm (the Cockerdene of many medieval documents) and then up to Liverpool Road. A long shallow ford crossed the river between Hutton and Lea and, although we must always be very wary of speculation, conceivably there was a metalled Roman ford over the river associated with the fort and small town at Kirkham. A document in the Cockersand cartulary mentions land in Hutton which belonged to 'the river guide of Lea', confirming that the crossing was of sufficient importance in the thirteenth century to have an 'official' guide, like the

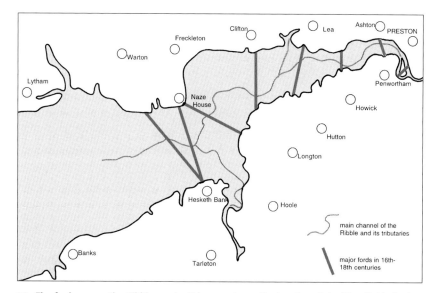

10. The fords across the Ribble sands. This map shows the location of the identifiable fords across the Ribble which existed in the period from about 1500 to 1800. These crossings were all in use in the Middle Ages as well, although not all are documented in that period, and they were a major element in the communications pattern of the region until the mid-nineteenth century, when the growth of the railway network and the dredging of the river led to their abandonment and disappearance.

better-known fords from Warton and Freckleton to Hesketh Bank and Tarleton. This significance of this crossing is further suggested by Dungeon Farm at its southern end. This distinctive name is found in several other places in Lancashire and Cheshire, each associated with an estuary crossing: for example, at Freckleton, at the northern end of the ford from Hesketh Bank; at Hale, at the end of the very long and dangerous sands crossing of the Mersey; and at Thurstaston on Wirral, from which the sands of Dee could be forded to North Wales. It is derived from the Middle English word *dongeon*, meaning a secure or guarded place. The crossings were used by men and horses, and probably also by wagons, but the ford could only be used at the lowest tides. The *dongeon* was therefore the place where the guide had his house and also a secure 'left luggage' room or lock-up for the goods awaiting the crossing.[45]

Notably absent from the landscape of medieval and sixteenth-century Hutton was woodland, of which only a few small areas seem to have survived into the Middle Ages. The largest was the wood at Cockerdene, which still survives in part. It is mentioned in a grant of land by Abel de Hutton to Cockersand in 1200x1236,[46] when it is described as being part of 'the land of St Cuthbert', an ambiguous phrase interpreted by some earlier historians as indicating that the land was owned by the parish church of Lytham, which is dedicated to that saint. Whether or not that is the case, the name Cockerdene (now altered to Cockerton) means 'the valley [*denu*] with the wood where the cocks [*coccu*] live', and it is not connected, except by coincidence, with the name Cockersand (the sands by the River Cocker). The only other wood mentioned in several of the deeds is Bradford Greaves, where the second part of the name is from the Old English *grafa* and is the same as the modern word *grove*. The word 'greave' is usually connected with a piece of woodland managed for its timber resources, and may in some circumstances indicate a deliberately-planted wood. The trees would be coppiced – that is, felled after about twenty years and then allowed to grow from the base with several new shoots instead of one main trunk. These shoots would be straight and even, ideal for making fenceposts, tool handles, and uprights in timber-framing for buildings. After perhaps fifteen years they would be cut again and the process repeated. Coppicing was the main renewable form of timber production in medieval England, found all over the country, and we have an example here in Hutton.[47]

8. *Bradford*

Bradford, the broad ford over the Mill Brook, has already been mentioned. It appears frequently in documentary sources of the thirteenth and fourteenth centuries and for a time was recognised as a place in its own right, distinct from (although within the boundaries of) Hutton. Thus, in 1230x1262 Cockersand was given two acres 'in the Bradford field'; in 1341 Cecily, widow of Robert of Horsford, quitclaimed to Thomas, son of John de Notscagh (Nutshaw), her 'properties in Bradford in the town of Hutton'; and in a deed of September 1348 Robert, son of Roger de Bradford is named, indicating that this was an identifiably separate locality. The reference to 'Bradford field' may mean that the hamlet had a small open arable field of its own.[48] However, Bradford never developed into a community in the modern sense, remaining as a farm and a few cottages. Eventually, its identity vanished altogether: it no longer appears in written sources after the sixteenth century, the ford was replaced by a bridge, and the name fell out of use. Perhaps its main distinction was that here was the watermill that served Hutton. We do not know when a mill was first constructed on the brook below the ford on Liverpool Road, but it was certainly well before 1200. At least 6000 watermills are recorded from different parts of England in the reign of William I so it is quite possible that the mill predated the Norman Conquest. The ownership of watermills was a manorial privilege, most manorial tenants being compelled to grind their corn at the lord's mill and also to pay *mulcture*, a 'tax' levied by the lord for the task. Mills were thus a valuable and jealously-protected property, and some of the earliest documents relating to the Cockersand estates concern the mill at Hutton. In the first decades of the thirteenth century the canons acquired the moiety, or half-share, in the mill which belonged jointly to the heirs of Roger de Howick, father-in-law of Elias de Hutton. The joint inheritors of this half were Roger's daughters, Sapientia, wife of Elias, and Helen, wife of Matthew. Cockersand eventually acquired the other half as well, from John de Clayton (le Woods) and his wife Avice (daughter of Warin de Walton) and from Roger de Noteschagh (Nut-shaw). Having secured full control of the mill, as well as the lordship of the manor, Cockersand took immediate steps to prevent others from challenging its monopoly on milling in the manor, by obtaining grants and quitclaims over all rights to operate mills, and to take waters for that purpose, on the two streams which formed the northern and southern boundaries of the township, 'the waters of Wymott and Bradford'.[49]

On the first edition of the Ordnance Survey six–inch map, surveyed in the mid-1840s, the mill itself is not shown, but Forest Mill Bridge is named, while Mill Brow Farm, then as now, stood a couple of hundred yards south of the crossing of the brook, on the west side of Liverpool Road. The name Forrest Mill (it should have two 'r's) is derived from Richard Forrest, who in November 1675 was granted a lease on the mill by Lawrence Rawstorne. The deed refers to the messuage (a legal term for a house) with 'that Water Corne-Mill and Kilne ... with all Milne-Fleams, Damms, Fenders & Calls ... and sufficient place and places for the Customers of the said Milne to winnow'. In June 1742, by another

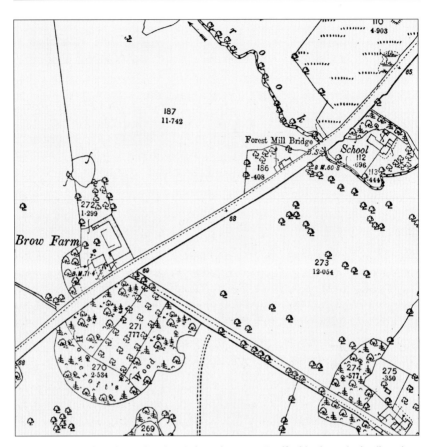

11. The area which in the medieval period was known as Bradford is shown in detail on the Ordnance Survey 25-inch to 1-mile map of 1895. Here we see the original line of the 1770 Preston and Liverpool turnpike road (now the dual-carriageway A59) crossing Mill Brook next to Howick School. This was the location of the original 'broad ford' and the medieval watermill, although by the late-nineteenth century both the ford and the mill had long since disappeared.

lease, the tenant of the mill, William Marten, sub-let the property to Thomas Mayer. In this document the mill is named: 'all that mill and kiln ... formerly or commonly called Forrest Mill and Kiln [with] two small crofts or parcels of ground adjoining, called the Mill Croft and the Kiln Croft ... as also the Gear in the said Miln, that is to say, The Lying Stone, the Running Stone and all other Utensills'.[50]

9. *The Rawstornes and Hutton Hall*

In the late 1530s the monastic control which Hutton had experienced for over three hundred years came to an abrupt end. The township, like many other places where a religious house had been the dominant influence, was henceforth dependent upon a secular landowner. Cockersand, with all other larger religious houses, was swept away under the second phase of the Dissolution. Its properties and assets were surrendered to the Crown in the autumn of 1539. Given the fact that for at least half a century the manor of Hutton had been leased to the Faringtons it is perhaps surprising that this important local gentry family did not then acquire the property outright, but instead the Cockersand manor and estates in Hutton became (after a few years in the hands of the Crown) the property of the Rawstorne family. The Rawstornes originated in, and took their surname from, Rostherne in north Cheshire, where they had estates in the twelfth century. One of the family, Richard de Rostherne, moved to Lumb, near Edenfield on the edge of Rossendale, and his descendant, Lawrence Rawstorne of New Hall in Edenfield, bought Hutton from the Crown, the transfer being confirmed by letters patent of Henry VIII dated 9 March 1546. Lawrence was also granted other properties, in Wrightington, Parbold, Bretherton, Shevington, Clayton-le-Woods, Cuerden, Croston and Longton, which had been Cockersand possessions, but despite the acquisition of these extensive estates, for several more generations his family considered New Hall and Edenfield as their main home. Thus, one of the most prominent members of the family, Lawrence Rawstorne (1619–1700) was usually described as 'of New Hall' rather than 'of Hutton'.[51]

For reasons which are not entirely clear, the Rawstornes did not retain the old grange, the site of the early medieval manor house, as their Hutton residence. Perhaps it was too decrepit and uncomfortable. Instead they built a new house (or perhaps made extensive alterations and improvements to an existing property) at Hutton Hall, on the edge of the moor in the centre of the township. This was certainly a more convenient location, as it lay close to the main road from Preston to Liverpool, and tradition has always maintained that the house (demolished in 1959–60) was built in the early years of the seventeenth century. The date 1634, found on a datestone built into the house, was often quoted, although there was no certainty that the stone was in its original location. Members of the family did live here, but Hutton was quite clearly the secondary residence and for much of the two centuries after 1546 was not normally occupied by the main branch of the Rawstornes. They were, therefore, semi-absentee lords of the manor, usually sub-letting the property to relatives who were *de facto* resident squires but who were not the owners of the estate. Thus in the reigns of James I and Charles I the occupant of the Hall was Peter Rawstorne, who is described in his will (1638) as a gentleman but who was not as personally wealthy as one or two of the larger tenant farmers, and was sufficiently ordinary to have acted as one of the valuers in making the inventory of John Martin, a husbandman (small farmer) who died in 1636.[52]

The Rawstornes were active in public life during the seventeenth and eighteenth centuries. Edward Rawstorne, great-grandson of the Lawrence who purchased the estate, was a leading Royalist during the Civil War and served as an officer in the heroic defence of Lathom House when it was besieged in 1644–45. He died in 1646, by which time his estates, including Hutton, had been sequestered (confiscated) by parliament. He had no surviving sons, and left three daughters as co-heirs, but the estates were granted to his brother, Lawrence, who (as though to illustrate the divisive effect of civil war) had been a leading supporter of the parliamentary cause. Lawrence Rawstorne retained the property, but after the Restoration made his peace with his old royalist foes and continued in public life, serving as high sheriff of Lancashire in 1681–82. His third wife was Margery, the daughter of John and Anne Fleetwood of Pen-wortham Priory, who had also been vigorous in their espousal of the parliament. This marriage tended to reinforce the place of Hutton and adjacent townships in the Rawstorne 'heritage', and although Lawrence maintained a close involvement in the affairs of Bury and Rossendale, in the years before his death he spent much time in and around Preston enjoying the company of his relatives, the Fleetwoods, and living for periods at Hutton Hall.

Nonetheless, a slightly detached attitude to Hutton continued through the eighteenth century. The Rawstornes had a town house in Preston, which made Hutton less attractive as a permanent residence since the town house was more convenient for Preston's social and cultural attractions. However, in 1806 Colonel Lawrence Rawstorne purchased Penwortham Priory and one of the two manors within the township of Penwortham, and after rebuilding the house in the years after 1815 he made it his main home. This at least gave him a much closer geographical connection with the contiguous Hutton estates, especially since he also bought Howick Hall and its lands. Lawrence was a well-known local figure, a great 'hunting squire'. One of his claims to immortality was that he wrote a book, *Gamonia*, which was concerned with management of game and shooting preserves and drew heavily upon his intimate personal knowledge of Penwortham, Howick and Hutton. It was illustrated with watercolours depicting local copses and covers. However, when Lawrence died in 1850 the family left Penwortham and it was leased to a succession of tenants.

Lawrence was, perhaps more than any other member of his family, a major presence in the affairs of Hutton. His diaries, which although incomplete span the years 1810–1849, recount in detail the implementation of his plans for the hall, where he had been living for some years. As work on the new house at Penwortham Priory progressed, he 'settled to enlarge the House at Hutton as a Residence for my Mother & Sisters, a plan in which they are all much interested with the exception of Mary Anne'. His architect drew up plans for major alterations, including 'A Drawing Room 25 × 19', an Eating Room 24 × 22½ with bedrooms over' at the east end. The comfort of his elderly mother was a priority: 'Great attention is to be paid to warmth on my Mother's account. The situation is certainly sheltered and there is fall sufficient [i.e. natural drainage] to make it dry'. He estimated that the cost would be well over £1,500 and proposed that when it was finished his mother would in exchange hand over to him the possession of the town house in Preston.[53] Work began in the summer of 1811, the furniture from the hall and the Preston house being taken to store at Penwortham, and a year later Lawrence wrote that 'the building at Hutton is much advanced and will be completed in a few weeks' time. The house will be a very good one, very convenient & look much better than I expected'. On 1 October 1812 he noted that 'the House at Hutton is now completed and appears most convenient in every respect and very well executed ... The marble chimney piece for the Drawing Room by one Napper in town is neatly designed and beautifully finished'. However, the final stages – decorating and making minor adjustments – lasted longer than anticipated and not until March 1813 was it possible for Mrs Rawstorne to move in. Lawrence, solicitous for her welfare, hoped that as 'so much attention has been paid to warmth in the building ... there is no reason why she may not remain there the winter in safety'. There were problems, but overall the project had been a success. In January 1814 he wrote in his journal that 'The Drawing Room is warm – the coldness of the dining room may proceed from the French windows, but on the whole

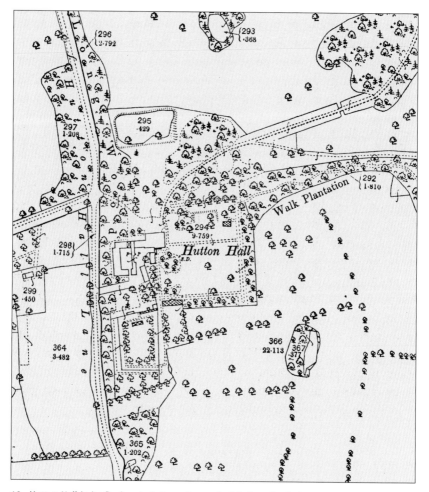

12. Hutton Hall in its final period of greatness, depicted on the Ordnance Survey 25-inch to 1-mile map of 1895: the map shows the wooded surroundings which made the area a popular destination for day-trippers in the 1920s and 1930s. South of the hall is the kitchen garden with greenhouses, and there are formal flower gardens and lawns to the east. The hall was finally demolished in the late 1950s when the new police headquarters was built on the site.

it appears to agree well with my mother'. At this point he calculated
the total cost of the work:

Roper [a builder] by contract	£734–14–10	
ditto for taking down and building up south side	£ 79–00–00	
various additions with chimney pieces and ceilings	£184–08–07	
		£998–03–05
Dandy [another builder] by contract	£626–00–00	
ditto for south side	£ 46–00–00	
		£672–00–00
Bricks with carting &c (say)	£200–00–00	£200–00–00
Total		£1,870–03–05

All this work, together with the even larger project under way two
miles down the road at Penwortham Priory, created grave financial
problems. In November 1815 he proposed 'shutting up Penwortham for
the winter. The house is so damp and cold that I intend living with
my mother, which will also be a saving as I have lived beyond my
income and am now in arrears to the Bank £2000'. As he estimated the
cost of the rebuilding of Penwortham as at least £8,000, even if materials
from the old house were reused, such belated caution was clearly a
necessity. As a result of this extensive rebuilding project the house at
Hutton was soon to become the family's main Lancashire home, for the
huge Gothic pile of Penwortham Priory was regarded by the next
generation as inconvenient and expensive, while the more modest and
more comfortable Hutton Hall was deemed acceptable. Even so, the
Rawstornes would only hold the manor and estates at Hutton for another
seventy years – the investment undertaken by Lawrence at such great
cost in the 1820s was eventually to prove a futile waste.

10. *Governing the Community*

So far we have paid particular attention to the landscape and economy
of Hutton, emphasising the manor and the estate. By the end of the

sixteenth century, though, a rudimentary local government system was beginning to evolve, and it is to the administration of the community that we can now turn. Until the late nineteenth century local government in the modern sense was largely absent, but a long sequence of parliamentary legislation over the previous three hundred years had gradually placed administrative responsibilities and duties upon the community. Hutton, in common with all other Lancashire places and with parishes and townships throughout England, was governed by a small number of officials appointed from among the ratepayers. These officials were unpaid and untrained, and were in theory volunteers, chosen from among their fellow-ratepayers at an annual meeting and with a one-year term of office. In reality most served with great reluctance, because unpaid burdens of this sort could be very irksome, even in a small and enclosed community such as Hutton where the scale of their work was relatively limited. The most prestigious local office was that of churchwarden, for these men were in regular contact with the squire and the vicar, and so had to be relatively important within the community, literate and socially-acceptable. Next in rank was the overseer of the poor, who managed the complex operation of the Poor Law and exercised a very considerable power over the lives of the less fortunate inhabitants. Then came the surveyor of the highways, whose job was as onerous or as unimportant as he chose to make it, depending on the attitude and vociferousness of his neighbours. People have complained about the state of the roads for many centuries, and a highway surveyor was on the receiving end of the earlier equivalents of the letters to the press and complaints to the council which are familiar today. Finally came the constable, who had the thankless task of trying to maintain at least some order in an unruly and often violent society, but was also involved in other aspects of social administration, such as checking that manorial regulations were followed and – most difficult of all, perhaps – collecting the taxes and rates, going from house to house and demanding money.

This system of local unpaid officials who served one-year terms evolved after the mid-sixteenth century and it lasted, in rural places such as Hutton, until the late nineteenth century. It was not until 1 January 1895 that democratically-elected parish councils came into existence, though in 1875 the rural sanitary authorities, the predecessors of rural district councils, were created. The system lasted for three centuries and it is therefore most unfortunate that for Hutton there are, as far as we can tell, no surviving local records to tell us of the work of these township officials. Some papers probably went up in flames when the vestry at Penwortham church was destroyed by fire in 1858, but most have presumably been accidentally lost or deliberately thrown away over the centuries. However, some evidence can be obtained from the records of the quarter sessions courts, because the county magistrates, the justices of the peace, exercised a supervisory and regulatory role in the affairs of individual communities, a role which was made compulsory under legislation of 1691.

Thus we learn that the ratepayers of Hutton informally chose two constables from among their number, their names being then approved by the manorial lord or his steward at a meeting of the court leet of the manor.[54] A rough but fair system operated, whereby each year individuals were chosen from a different section of the township in turn. This method was indicated in 1654 when Henry Longton and Richard Maire were ordered to be constables 'as they ought to do it coming to them by house row' – that is, each group of dwellings provided the officials by rotation.[55] These procedures emphasise the powerful role of the lords of the manor, the Rawstorne family, in the affairs of the community. In the past the constable had everywhere been a manorial officer, but in many places the manor had ceased to enjoy any direct involvement in his appointment by the mid-seventeenth century. At Hutton, though, the tradition of manorial domination and control died hard. The importance of the meeting of the manor court and of the lord's presence is highlighted by events in the early 1650s. The constables, Rafe Loxham and Richard Mayre, served their year's term which ended at Whitsun 1650 and were due to be replaced at the meeting of the court leet but, as they told the justices in a petition of complaint, 'the lord of the township being at Longton the Court missed and [was] held not'. The non-sitting of the court therefore meant that Loxham and Mayre were not replaced, and they had to ask the steward to make alternative arrangements. He obtained the permission of Lawrence Rawstorne to appoint successors, John Martin and Roger Bamber, who were described as 'sufficient men as we all know for constables'. However, Martin and Bamber refused to take the oath of office, because they had not been appointed in open court, and eventually the magistrates had to order them to appear at the quarter sessions in Ormskirk, in the second week of July, and take the oaths, which they duly did.[56]

In 1652 there were further problems with the appointment of the constables, and the correct procedures were carefully recited in a petition to the magistrates. William Mawdesley and Robert Mayor, constables for 1651–1652, claimed on 17 January 1653 that they had 'executed their office for that whole year and have made and given up just account to the assessors thereof' – in other words, had completed the annual accounts and handed them with the balance of cash to the ratepayers for unofficial audit. It was, they said, 'a Custom in Hutton that the Constables of the same, are Chosen by Lawrence Rawstorne of the New Hall Esquire (being Lord of the Manor thereof) or by his Bailiff by him appointed'. According to Mawdesley and Mayor the newly-appointed steward, John Forrest, had ('his Master putting him in trust') selected Hugh Waring and Raphe Milner to be constables for 1652–1653, 'which Office [they] not only neglect but absolutely deny it and say they will not serve but by plain Force'. The present constables complained that as a result they 'abide still undischarged of their office to their great Losses and hindrance'. Wasting no time, the magistrates ordered Waring and Milner to conform and on 21 January they went to Wigan to swear the oath of office before Richard Standish.[57]

This was perhaps a storm in a teacup, but it illustrates the importance placed upon correct procedures and the careful supervision of these appointments by the manor and the magistracy. It helped, of course, that Lawrence Rawstorne was himself a prominent magistrate, for in the somewhat blatant fashion of the seventeenth century he could use his influence to try to ensure that matters involving Hutton and his estates were given the full attention of the bench. However, we may also observe an undercurrent in local society. Despite the power and influence of the lord and his courts, some people at least were defiant and resented being ordered about in this fashion. The manorial system was not universally popular, especially at this time of extreme social and political turbulence.

Crime was not a major problem in seventeenth- and eighteenth-century Hutton, not because rural communities in this period were necessarily law-abiding and peaceful – far from it, for by modern standards this was a seriously lawless society – but because the dominance of the Rawstornes represented a powerful influence in favour of good behaviour. A strong manorial lord and an assiduous and effective steward could between them ensure that the tenants of a manor (in Hutton's case, most of the inhabitants) toed the line. If they did not, they faced penalties such as loss of tenancy and eviction. Therefore, although almost no crimes in Hutton came before the quarter sessions, there were undoubtedly minor offences dealt with by local impromptu retribution or by the steward of the manor. The only 'official' crime in Hutton in the whole of the seventy years from 1630 was an alleged case of sheep-stealing, a common offence in this period. In 1639 Robert Mayor bought a sheep on Preston market at Whitsuntide and put it on the marsh at Hutton to graze with the flock belonging to Hugh Worthington. Mayor did not have grazing rights of his own, but Worthington, who did, was paid a small sum to include the beast in his own flock. The sheep disappeared at Shrovetide (mid-February) 1640 and at Eastertime Mayor was told that the animal was now on Longton Marsh, with a different mark upon her. Maybe, though, even this was not outright theft, for an animal could wander with ease from Hutton Marsh to Longton, where it was perhaps seen as a gift of Providence.[58]

Hutton people probably suspected that a lot of crime that was committed was undertaken by outsiders – such as foreigners from Longton. There was, as everywhere else, a deep suspicion of anybody not from the immediate locality, and strong social pressure was placed upon individuals who did not conform or refused to uphold the rules which society defined. Free spirits and nonconformists (whether in the religious or the behavioural sense) were unwelcome. An instance of such pressure in action is seen in a letter written by Lawrence Rawstorne to John Harrington, a fellow-magistrate and distant relative, in January 1695, concerning a Hutton woman: 'you will have some complaint from William Read's wife, a person that would be troublesome to her neighbours, being of a turbulent unquiet spirit and very vexatious, not with her husband only but all others about her, receive no encouragement but rather reprove her. You'll never be at quiet else'. A comparable attempt to influence the deliberations of the magistrates occurred in 1693, when Rawstorne wrote to Alexander Kenyon, the clerk of the peace, reporting that Thomas Mayre of Hutton was so 'imperious ... that the officers are Kept in awe by him and tells them that he cares not for them or me'. He suggested to Kenyon that if Thomas Mayre came to the Ormskirk sessions asking the justices for more money, ''tis my desire they either regard him not or mitigate [reduce] his allowance as the best expedient to curb his proud spirit'. It is clear that those who did not show suitable deference to the lord might well suffer accordingly.[59]

II. *Managing the Poor*

Thus, we can envisage Hutton before the nineteenth century as a peaceful but not uniformly contented society, a place where although serious crime was exceptionally rare and manorial regulation invariably strong, life was not necessarily idyllic. For many, indeed, life was extremely hard. Hutton had its fair share of the poor, the disadvantaged and those whose lot in life was miserable and distressing. How did the system cope with them and how did it treat them? Under laws passed in the last years of Elizabeth's reign the deserving poor, such as orphans, the very old and the physically disabled, who were deemed to be paupers through no fault of their own, were to be supported by the community with financial help, usually known as poor relief and funded by the rates. The undeserving poor – able-bodied men in particular – were in contrast to be chastised and punished for their fecklessness. Legislation of 1598 and 1601 made the parish the administrative unit for the Poor Law, but this caused serious problems in northern England because of the nature of its parish system. Amending legislation in 1662 made the township the administrative unit in the northern counties, and also codified the concept of 'settlement', whereby every pauper legally belonged to a specific place which was liable for his or her maintenance. Thus, until 1662 the parish of Penwortham and the township of Hutton had a joint but uncertain responsibility for the poor of Hutton, whereas after 1662 the township alone was involved.

The overseers of the poor were in charge of all matters relating to the Poor Law and its operation, but in some circumstances paupers could petition the magistrates for redress if they felt aggrieved by the behaviour or decision of the overseer (who could, in turn, counter-petition) while on occasion the overseers or the township collectively might ask the magistrates for a legal decision about a confused or ambiguous case. The papers which survive among the quarter sessions records give us our only insight into the Poor Law in Hutton, three hundred years of overseers' papers being apparently lost. The human tragedies and pitiful cases which the magistrates considered emphasise, if emphasis were needed, that we should not assume that all was always well. Yet we may also note a genuine sense of concern for the plight of at least some of the poor. Although ratepayers loathed paying high rates, and were fearful of commitments which increased Hutton's public expenditure (a phenomenon which is well nigh universal) there was an occasional awareness of the social responsibilities of the community. In 1656, for example, fifteen leading ratepayers in Hutton signed a petition to the magistrates:

> There is one Grace Martin in the House of Correction [in Preston] and hath been a quarter of a year and hath three small children almost starved both for lack of meat and clothes and dressing which formerly the said Grace their mother hath keeped the children in a better condition and would do again if the said Grace their mother could be released, and we whose names are under written do humbly desire your good worships that the said Grace might be released.[60]

The more cynical might note, however, that, apart from considerations of kindness, the ratepayers would have to support the three children using the poor rate if the mother remained in prison, so perhaps self-interest and humanity coincided in this instance. The loss of records means that we do not know how many paupers were 'on the books' in Hutton at any one time, how much they were paid, for how long, or why. We only see the cases where disagreement led to the matter coming before the justices, and this may give us a distorted perspective. We also ought to acknowledge that, human nature being what it is, the petitions to the magistrates exaggerated the plight of the individuals for dramatic and heart-tugging effect. Nonetheless, some of the cases do seem to particularly distressing and some dragged on for years, the overseers and the magistrates hardening their hearts and the paupers' circumstances not improving.

In the case of Mary Bamber, for example, the overseers were reluctant to assist because she was not born in Hutton. She petitioned the magistrates in 1658, stating that her husband John, whom she had married over three years previously, was a native of Hutton and they had a son who was now a year and a half old. Her husband then deserted her, 'having left her and his little son without any means of subsistence they are exposed to misery and she is constrained to betake herself to service'. She asked for help from the township of Hutton to maintain the child

until she could find work, but the overseers and magistrates refused. In
1661 she again sought help, pointing out that her husband was from
Hutton, that he had 'gone your petitioner knows not whither', and that
she had endeavoured to look after the child although she was 'miserably
poor [but now] things are so dear and scarce that she by her labours is
not able to maintain herself and her said child, and she would fain not
beg'. The response of the magistrates was laconic and unsympathetic:
'Mother and grandmother to keep it'. Another attempt was made in
1662, when her petition emphasised the harshness of the world, for the
people of Hutton did not want this 'stranger' in their midst even though
the child was the son of a Hutton man. Mary stated that she had worked
to maintain the boy, had gone into service, and had done her best
without any assistance from Hutton, but 'now so it is the said inhabitants
will not permit [her] to bring her said infant into the same town,
although the grandmother of the said child of her proper costs and
charges would maintain and keep it during her life'. The magistrates
finally conceded at least this point, and ordered the overseers of Hutton
to let the boy live with his grandmother in the township.[61]

There were other pitiful cases. In 1661 Margaret Tuson, a young
widow, petitioned on behalf of herself and her five 'poor fatherless
children'. In contrast to Mary Bamber she had 'inhabited all her life
time in Penwortham parish in the town of Hutton' but, because of her
circumstances, was now 'destitute of habitation and very likely to be
starved by lying out of doors and her children are very like to be famished
for want of food and relief'. She asked to be housed and to be given
relief (i.e. financial assistance from the poor rate) and in this instance,
her credentials presumably being good, the magistrates instructed the
overseer to provide for the family.[62] In 1664 there were several contentious
cases. Robert Miller, his wife and two children were 'very impotent'
(helpless) and the justices took pity on them, requiring that Hutton
should immediately pay them relief at the rate of one shilling (5p) per
week. However, the overseer objected and the magistrates quickly back-
tracked, deferring a final judgment until a later meeting.[63]

Margery Martin or Marton, spinster, described as a 'poor, lame and
infirm person', was crippled from birth or childhood. She was born in
Hutton and looked after by her father, on whose death responsibility
for her upkeep passed to her brother Robert. He then married and had
children, which so increased his expenses so that, as she told the magis-

trates, he 'hath turned your poor petitioner out of doors, but that her good neighbours doth relieve her, and is like to come to extreme misery except you help [her]'. The justices were unswayed and recorded their verdict on her: 'nothing'. It was considered that her brother should have the obligation to maintain his sister: whether he actually did so was not the concern of the magistrates or of the overseers, but only of his conscience. In desperation she appealed again for help, and the magistrates this time decided that the township of Hutton should provide for her. However, the overseers refused to give her anything except 'some small sum of money to pay for [her] diet and never offered to provide her any apparel or such other necessaries'. A third petition was therefore made in 1665, when she was said to be 'decrepit and lame and not able to get herself any livelihood by her own labour nor hath anything wherewith to maintain herself save only what charitable people bestow upon her'. The magistrates, mindful of the fact that their previous order had been largely ignored, ordered the overseer of Hutton to provide for all her needs, including clothing.[64]

We can see in cases such as these an inherent conflict in policy towards the poor, in Hutton as in every other place. The poor could only be assisted by monetary payments funded by the rates, and the ratepayers wanted to minimise expenditure. There was thus little scope for giving people the benefit of the doubt, or for sentiment or obvious compassion. The overseers, ratepayers themselves, were ever conscious that each time they agreed to give help, the rates might go up. In a small community such as Hutton a commitment to even one or two more paupers could materially affect the expenditure of the community. In 1664 Hugh Waring and Henry Strickland, the overseers, made a formal complaint to the magistrates, claiming that they 'do believe and can find out [prove] that there are several persons within Hutton ... which hath allowance [from] the town that are not in any wise needful of relief or allowance', meaning that the magistrates had ordered them to help individuals who were not genuinely deserving of assistance. They listed the cases: Anne Tuson, widow, 'hath sufficient means or estate of her own and ought not to have relief of the town'; Margery Marton could be looked after by her brother; Ellen Bamber 'sets forth money to use' (lends money to other people) 'and needeth no allowance'; and in the case of Robert Milner, the grandfather has money and means to support his son and grandchildren. The magistrates, naturally giving great weight to the views of the ratepayers and overseers, ordered Anne Tuson's allowance to be stopped, Margery Marton to be lodged with her brother and only helped if he refused to do so, Ellen Bamber to be looked after by her daughter who is able-bodied and had assets of £10, and Robert Milner's father to take care of his family.[65]

But of course, no matter how much the overseers might be ruthless in cutting out expenditure, and regardless of the views of the magistrates, poverty and the plight of individuals continued. Some cases were clear-cut and required little debate, but others dragged on wearily without resolution and with futile argument on both sides. No case highlights this more powerfully than that of a determined elderly lady, Ellen Eccleston or Edleston (they could not agree on the spelling of her name), a widow who had lived in Hutton since about 1667. She claimed in January 1675 that her daughter had been visited by 'the evil' ('king's evil' or scrofula) and that she herself, aged and partially blind, had been receiving five shillings a year in relief from the township. The overseer had stopped the payments, justifying his action because, he said, she was 'of ability to relieve herself, she having several very good goods of her own besides the said allowance, and her own daughter is a school mistress who gets much money by teaching the school'. The justices agreed with him that five shillings a year was quite sufficient in the circumstances. A year later, after another petition, Ellen was granted ten shillings a year, but on complaint from the overseer this was speedily halved to the previous figure. She did not come from Hutton, yet appeared to have a good claim to be supported by the township. Why was that so? In normal circumstances we would probably never know, but Ellen told more of her story to the magistrates in 1676:

the town or some of the town of Hutton where she is an inhabitor did bring her thither and promised her by way of encouragement that her daughter should teach school, which proved of no advantage [for] her daughter was by the white ague [tuberculosis] brought to impotence and lowness, and this aged woman was forced to travel many a mile to gather the relief of well-disposed people, the town not willing to relieve her at all and she having another daughter which would have been some succour to them in their said condition, they [the town] would give her no rest till she was banished from her old mother into Ireland and now her daughter which was thus lame being restored to health could not quietly be allowed in the town but is fled away and gone, and … this poor old woman in the midst of her succourless sorrow … cannot now travel, and is fourscore, and left childless and friendless and helpless.

She was given further help by order of the justices, but this soon lapsed. In 1681 she submitted a long petition to the magistrates, recounting in vivid detail the pitiful state in which she found herself, and also telling the harsh response of the local officials:

a poor aged woman, who is fourscore years of age at least, and unable for her living by reason of want of sight with other infirmities is not able to subsist, she having been an inhabiter in the town of Hutton fourteen years and hath demeaned herself honestly among them, being to her power laborious [hard-working] as one of that age could be, and now hath no certain house to dwell in, therefore she desires the honourable Bench to look upon her distressed condition and for the Lord's sake under God, to stand her friend; for … the overseer got her order [from the magistrates] by a while and said he would light tobacco with it, and would but give her half what the justices allowed her, and since then she hath been forth to seek relief in other towns or else she might have been lost, but for relief out of 'Farinton Midlforth and Penardom', she had been lost, therefore she begs of you, intreats and beseeches your worships' favour, to stand her friend to grant her an order where by she may have some relief according to what your worships' favour thinks fit for such an old and impotent creature and an house to dwell in.

The magistrates investigated and found that Ellen was being given five shillings a year, was genuinely unable to fend for herself, and had originally lived at Charnock Richard before being 'invited' to live in Hutton. They ordered the overseers of Hutton to provide relief, but to no avail. The officers of the township were determined not to pay for an incomer with only fourteen years' residence, and so tried to get rid of the problem. When in 1683 she tried yet again to obtain help she revealed the ploy which 'the Towns men of Hutton' had attempted. They 'gave her twenty shillings & some 3 or 4 Shillings more, to avoid the town' – to go somewhere else – and, taking the money, off she went, hoping to go towards the south (probably the Wigan area which was her homeland) but because of her weak, blind and elderly state could not manage to keep herself. She was therefore 'Tossed from place to place' and finally ended up in Hutton again. The magistrates, maybe exasperated by the way in which their previous instruction had been ignored, ordered the overseer of Hutton to look after Ellen. Let us hope that, at last, he did so.[66]

In all this it must be said that the overseers of Hutton, unlike their counterparts in many larger and more open communities, had their hands tied by the dominant influence of the landowner, who exerted constant pressure to restrict the expenditure on poor relief, because he paid by far the largest contribution to the rates. In 1688 Lawrence Rawstorne wrote a letter to Roger Kenyon, the clerk of the peace, lamenting his personal financial loss from this cause and asking for action to be taken: 'Hutton, one of the towns within the parish of Penwortham, is so burdened with their poor [and] is not at all eased by the rest [of the townships] notwithstanding they have no poor, some of them, and the rest not in any equality … If you think it feasible, pray you promote that the parish may be charged mutually to contribute with it … and it will be a great kindness to us, for the greatest share lies indeed upon me'.[67] Rawstorne wanted the whole parish, rather than the individual townships, to pay for the poor of Hutton, so that his personal costs would be reduced. This would, however, have meant Hutton contributing to the relief of the poor of other, larger, places such as Penwortham and Longton, and was also have been entirely contrary to the statute of 1662 which made townships legally responsible for their own poor. In this matter at least, his local influence made no difference at all – the law stood and the request was fruitless. But the letter exemplifies the attitude of the man who was by far the most powerful figure within this community. It surely would have been a brave, perhaps a very unwise, overseer who was considered by Rawstorne to be over-generous to the paupers in his care.

All over this part of Lancashire in the late eighteenth and early nineteenth centuries the attitudes to the poor on the part of the authorities were changing. The provision of places in workhouses, rather than the practice of relieving paupers who stayed in their own homes, became more common. At Longton the township built a workhouse for its paupers in 1821, while at Penwortham the workhouse at Middleforth

13. The Hutton township workhouse was built in 1827, on land given by Lawrence Rawstorne. Today a private residence, it is named Rawstorne House in commemoration of the benefactor and his family.

Green was opened in 1796. In Hutton the township authorities built the new workhouse in Pope Lane (known until the early twentieth century as Workhouse Lane) in 1827. The building still exists, converted into a house, and is a remarkable tribute to the ambitions of a small township. It is of brick, with stone dressings and slate roof, rectangular in plan and of three storeys including the basement, which is half above ground level. The building is made especially imposing by the double flight of brick steps in the centre, leading to an impressive stone-framed doorway. The reason for this architectural ambition – far more than would normally be expected in a place of the size of Hutton – is given on the inscribed tablet between the windows diagonally above the door:

This Work House was erected in the year 1827 at the Expense of the Tax Payers of the Township of Hutton. The Foundation & Area consisting of 1106 square yards. Given by Law. Rawstorne Esq.

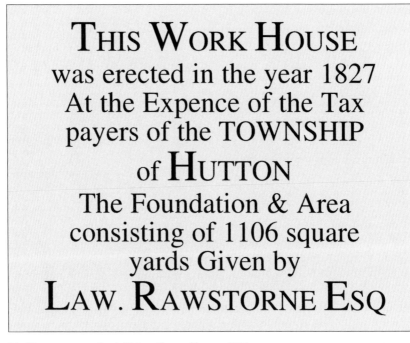

THIS WORK HOUSE
was erected in the year 1827
At the Expence of the Tax
payers of the TOWNSHIP
of HUTTON
The Foundation & Area
consisting of 1106 square
yards Given by
LAW. RAWSTORNE ESQ

14. The commemorative tablet on the workhouse, 1827.

Here, as in so many other ways, the Rawstornes left their mark upon Hutton. The generosity and public-spiritedness of Lawrence Rawstorne elevated the workhouse of a modest rural township into the realms of architecture, and it remains today as a splendid example of the local workhouses of the last decades of the Old Poor Law. Why was such an impressive building needed? As is explained in more detail below, the population of Hutton grew exceptionally rapidly during the first thirty years of the nineteenth century, and although this growth was fuelled mainly by the employment opportunities represented by handloom weaving, there is no doubt that there were significantly more paupers in the township in 1830 than there had been in 1790. The same pattern certainly applied to Penwortham and Longton as well. Ratepayers, worried by the growth in expenditure on the poor and concerned by the increase in numbers, sought new solutions to the problem. Ironically, only seven years after the Hutton workhouse was opened, the government passed the Poor Law Amendment Act which effectively removed the Poor Law powers exercised by the individual communities. All parishes and townships were compulsorily amalgamated into Poor Law Unions, covering large areas and centred on market towns and urban centres. Hutton and its neighbours were included within the new Preston Poor Law Union, which was administered by a new Board of Guardians on which Hutton had one representative. By 1840 the Preston Union was closing the township workhouses and eventually it replaced them with the great workhouse on Watling Street Road in Fulwood, which accommodated 1500 paupers. The Hutton workhouse was sold and converted into a farm, after a short life of less than twenty years as a public building.[68]

12. *Charities and Education*

The alternative form of help for the poor was charity, and in some places this represented a substantial contribution to the relieving of poverty. In Hutton, however, the sums available for charitable help were very small. Charities were established by or maintained by public bene-factors, great or small, whose sense of social responsibility and compassion for their less fortunate fellows moved them to make provision for their improvement. In 1704, for example, Edward Fleetwood of Penwortham gave £45 to be invested and the revenue used for the benefit of the poor of the township of Hutton. This produced an income of £2 per annum, while at some date shortly before then Richard Forrest of Forrest's Mill gave £20, generating a revenue of £1 a year, to be spent on gifts of beef for the poor of Hutton. Such tiny and purely local charities were legion in seventeenth- and eighteenth-century England. They were a modest acknowledgement by the benefactors of their own good fortune, but unfortunately they were often poorly administered or were abused for selfish non-charitable purposes by those nominally empowered to manage them. When the Charity Commissioners investigated the Hutton charities in 1825 they could find no documents relating to these two bequests, the administration of which was confused and chaotic.

They also recorded another legacy, £70 given by 'George Merry', which was likewise undocumented: indeed, the name of the benefactor is probably the ubiquitous Hutton surname Mayor or Maire, the error arising because the lack of written evidence meant that the investigators relied on oral testimony. Finally, the Commissioners noted with more precision that Thomas Marton had, by his will of December 1793, given £50 to generate an income for distribution among poor householders of Hutton who did not receive any relief from the township (the term used was 'the industrious poor who keep themselves off the town') together with another £20 to be used to buy beef to distribute among the poor on Christmas Eve. He also left £50 to increase the annual income of the minister or curate of Longton. Taking all these Hutton charities together, the Commissioners reported that an annual income in 1825 of £9 15s. 6d. (perhaps £2,300 in today's values) had been raised, this being distributed partly in beef (£2) and partly in sums of money ranging from one shilling (5p) to six shillings (30p). Even in the 1820s, this hardly represented riches, since the payments for a family from the poor rate might amount to several shillings a week.[69]

Much the largest charity affecting Hutton was not directly connected with poor relief but with education. To many people in Lancashire today Hutton is known for its institutions – the former agricultural college, the police headquarters and – far older than those – the grammar school, in origin a charitable foundation of the reign of Edward VI. That there was a grammar school in the township was a matter of historical accident, for the school was intended to serve the whole of Penwortham parish and during its first two centuries it was located at Longton. It was founded by Christopher Walton, probably the nephew of the William Walton who was priest at Longton chapel in the reign of Henry VIII. William had already endowed a chantry chapel there, among the duties of its priest being the teaching of grammar to poor local children. Chantries were abolished under the second stage of the Reformation in 1549, but in September 1552 Christopher Walton re-founded the original endowment to provide for a body of trustees – John Fleetwood, Peter Farington, James Forshaw and ten others – who would administer extensive lands in Preston, Kellamergh near Warton, and Kirkham and use the rent income from the property to pay a teacher to instruct young people in grammar and catechism. The teaching was to be free of charge for any child dwelling in the parish of Penwortham, and the school was to be in a convenient place within the parish: because it grew from the chapel school in Longton it continued there.[70]

The lands granted for the endowment of the grammar school are listed in detail in the first report of the Charity Commissioners, made in August 1825. They include properties in Hutton and Longton which were not part of the original benefaction, but were granted subsequently by Christopher Walton and his son John. The list of lands held by the school trustees in 1825 was almost identical with that of two hundred years before: in Preston, nine cottages and houses in Fishergate and Church Street, with almost forty parcels of land and other properties scattered through the town, and three pubs in Church Street – the *Horse Shoe*, the *Holy Lamb* and the *Blue Bell.* These town properties brought in an annual rent in 1825 of £568, which in modern terms is approaching £150,000, a figure which was likely to increase further as more land was let as building plots. In addition to these very valuable endowments, the trustees also had an income of £105 from cottages and houses in Kirkham; £54 from agricultural land and cottages in Longton; and £5 from 'two closes called Chapel Lands' in Hutton itself. There was also a smallholding in Hutton which had hitherto been let rent-free to the schoolmaster, and two pews in Longton chapel which were let out for small rents each year. The total income was thus about £830 per annum in the early 1820s, but the Charity Commissioners reported that the letting of the land had been mismanaged in the past, because the full

15. Penwortham Grammar School moved from Longton to a new site and new buildings at Hutton in 1746–47. This photograph (taken in 1931) shows what had by then become the old buildings of the school, almost two hundred years old. There had been internal alterations and some new windows inserted during the nineteenth century, but the basic appearance of the school was much as it had been for a century and a half. (LRO Library 405/76/004)

potential of the development sites within Preston had not been realised, and the agricultural lettings were on terms unduly favourable to the tenant.[71]

In the mid-1740s the trustees had accepted that the situation of the school, at the western end of the parish, was inconvenient, and the accommodation was in any case quite inadequate. The school was held in a small cottage adjacent to the chapel at Longton, but as the population of the area was growing it was clearly desirable to provide better facilities. In addition, the endowment funds seem to have been comparatively healthy at this stage and so the trustees could purchase a sizeable alternative site and construct new school buildings. They bought several acres of land on the south side of the main road between Preston and Longton, in Hutton township, and a schoolroom and house for the master were built there in 1746–47. The new site was not only more convenient but also had plenty of room for expansion. Even before this date, though, educational provision locally had been improved by the building of the little village school at Howick, founded in 1727 on land which had previously been part of Howick Moor. It, too, was an endowed school, although the value of its land was only £20 per annum. It took children from Howick township free of charge, but it could also take children from other townships including Hutton provided that their parents paid school fees. Subsequently a village charity school was re-founded in Longton itself, so that by 1800 the educational provision of the district was comparatively good.

13. *House, Money and Goods: Lifestyles in Seventeenth-century Hutton*

For some of the poor, therefore, educational opportunities were available, but we know very little about the detailed running of the school before the nineteenth century. Similarly, the daily lives of the poor and ordinary people of Hutton are virtually unknown to us, unless they came up against the system and appeared in quarter sessions records. Otherwise they appear only as names and dates in the transcripts of the Penwortham parish registers – though from that source there are two unexpected glimpses of how local people may have regarded each other. In March 1640 Henry Mayer of Hutton was buried at Penwortham and the clerk noted his highly uncomplimentary nickname – 'fat-back' – while a fortnight later Richard Wilding, usually known as 'Horrible Dick', was also buried there. We do, however, have evidence about the lifestyles of some of their more prosperous contemporaries. Wills and probate inventories give valuable insights into levels of domestic comfort and furnishings, and can shed light upon the farming activities of the community in the seventeenth and eighteenth centuries. Thus, the inventory of the possessions of Mary Mayer, widow, who died in November 1675, reveals the modest level of comfort which she enjoyed. Though she was better off than the poor of the township her household goods, clothes and other assets were worth in total only £8 11s. 6d. (£8.57). She had very little furniture – some bedding and (it is not listed but we can assume its existence) a wooden bedstead; some chests for storage; a couple of pots of pewter and brass; a few earthenware vessels; and a miscellany of chairs, stools and cushions. Most of her tableware and kitchen equipment was of wood, and she had a fire iron, a spit and a few other bits of cooking equipment. A relative by marriage, George Maire, died in December 1670 leaving goods worth £14 5s. 6d. (£14.27), and he too had small amounts of brass and pewter, some vessels of earthenware and wooden items, fire irons, a crow (or iron lever used to swing pots over the fire), and a griddle. His inventory lists 'Chares stules and one ould table', as well as a 'tressl' (i.e. a trestle table), 'shites and linnen'. It is clear that such people, who were smallholders also owning a few animals and a small area of crops, lived frugal and modest lives, without any luxury and, to our eyes, in no great comfort. Their houses had few furnishings, no curtains, carpets or rugs, and a minimum of bedlinen. They did not have separate kitchens – all living and cooking and indeed perhaps the sleeping was done in one room, the firehouse or hall in which was situated the only hearth.[72]

In contrast, Robert Maire, who died in 1673, was a prosperous yeoman farmer with goods valued at £398 8s. 2d. (£398.41). His will refers proudly to the family heirlooms which he passed on to his son John: 'a Longe Table a meale chist in the Chamber belowe, a greate brasse pott', and the inventory lists many items of household and kitchen equipment as well as soft furnishings and clothing. Earlier in the century Jennet or Joan Marton, who died in 1609, was the widow of a substantial yeoman farmer and her inventory also reflects a comfortable and substantial lifestyle. She had a fine range of brassware – three great pans, six little pans, five pots, a chafing dish (for keeping food warm), a brass ladle and a brass 'chandleer' or candlestick. There were, on the shelves of her buttery, fifteen pewter dishes, six pewter poddingers (small bowls), and a pewter saucer. The hearth, where the cooking was done, had a griddle, a spittle (a large flat shovel for use in cooking), a spit with its gabirons or supports, a pair of pothooks for hanging cauldrons on a chain above the fire, and a brandreth or large trivet to place over the fire for resting pans. She had a variety of specialised wooden equipment, including a churn and several bowls and dishes. Her living area was comfortably provided with cushions, and when she made up her two beds she could choose from an abundance of linen and covers: in the house when she died were twelve coverlets, four blankets, four featherbeds, a feather bolster, two feather pillows and a mattress and four bolsters filled with chaff, or straw. John Harrison alias Hughes (died 1623) was a small farmer, and had rather less comfort at home, but nonetheless he had a good variety of iron cooking and hearth equipment, a table and a dishboard (forerunner of a sideboard), a griddle, two frying pans, a hatchet and a cresset or oil lamp, while, exhausted by their labours, he and his wife could retire to bed (there were six beds in the house) warmed on cold winter nights by some of the two featherbeds, six feather bolsters, eleven coverlets and five blankets, one chaff mattress and three chaff bolsters. For some, at least, life could be reasonably comfortable even by modern standards.

At the top of the social scale were the Rawstornes, whose standard of living fitted their status as minor county gentry. Since the main branch of the family continued to live in Rossendale in the early seventeenth century, the occupants of Hutton Hall were usually socially junior relatives, but nonetheless they had a higher status (though not always greater wealth) than anyone else in Hutton. Status was only partly the result of income: birth and heredity were at least as important in measuring one's place in society. Peter Rawsthorne died in 1638, leaving goods valued at £184. The detailed list of the contents of his house gives telling evidence of his place in society, for he had 'ceiled [panelled] beds and bedstocks with hangings and curtains' – in other words, a four-poster – but most of his other possessions would have been equally appropriate for a yeoman farmer.

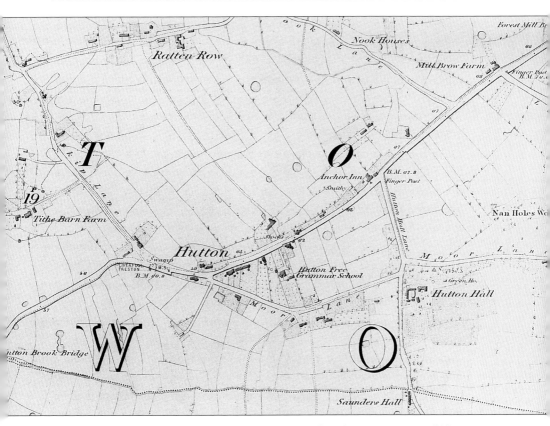

16. Hutton village in 1845: an extract from the 6-inch to 1-mile Ordnance Survey map which gives us the first really detailed picture of the township. It shows a pattern of scattered cottages and farms which had been relatively unaltered for several hundred years, although the population increase and prosperity which handloom weaving brought in the thirty years after 1800 had led to the building of small new cottages in the area of Hutton Row.

The parish of Hutton has only a few listed buildings and not much surviving evidence of the houses in which lived the testators described in this section. The 1994 list, prepared by the then Department of National Heritage, includes the following: Nutters Platt Farmhouse, in Lindle Lane; Hutton Manor, in Moor Lane; the former township workhouse in Pope Lane; the farmhouse, no. 150 Ratten Lane; and the two cottages at 138 and 140 Ratten Lane, a total of just six properties (though it should be noted that in the same listing the much larger parish of Penwortham had only twelve properties). The listing process, although subject to frequent revision, excludes the not inconsiderable number of 'ordinary' properties which, though recognisably old and retaining fea-

17. Mayor's Farm in Moor Lane, photographed in about 1900. This is the house which is now called Hutton Manor.

tures of architectural interest, are not deemed to have sufficient significance on a more than purely local scale. It is thus not a complete listing of all older buildings – for example, the oldest parts of the grammar school date from the mid-eighteenth century, when the school itself was founded on the present site. The buildings were greatly altered and extended in the later nineteenth century, and there have been many subsequent changes, so that architecturally and historically the structures have not as yet been regarded as worthy of listed status.[73] Likewise, at Bottom of Hutton there are several farm buildings and cottages of eighteenth- and nineteenth-century date which are not at present listed. Thus, the farmhouse and some outbuildings at Old Grange include evidence of early eighteenth-century work, and are of hand-made brick.

Most notable of the listed buildings, perhaps, is Hutton Manor in Moor Lane, which was apparently constructed in 1690. The initials on the inscription over the porch are *M I M R 1690*, and stand for Isobel,

18. Nutters Platt Farmhouse, at the junction of Lindle Lane and Pope Lane: although now considerably altered, the farmhouse was built in 1653 (according to the inscription carved on the lintel of the main doorway).

Robert and Mary Mayer (or Mair). The house is of brick, with a slate roof, and although its is changed in detail – the front windows, for example, have been replaced in the past century – there are original mouldings above the windows and some of the rear windows are also typical of the late seventeenth century. The interior is well preserved and this property is now among the best, in historical and architectural terms, of any in the parish. It should be noted, though, that this was never in fact the manor house; the present name is a recent one and has no historical authenticity. Another is the farmhouse at Nutters Platt, which is older (with a datestone and inscription of 1653: WILLIAM MODS LE BVLDED THIS HOVS. AD 1653: 'William Mawdesley built this house'), although it too has undergone a number of external changes. The cottages at 138 and 140 Ratten Lane are cruck-framed, and may date from the early seventeenth century, although extensive modernisation has taken place and externally it is not immediately obvious that the buildings are of such an age and architectural construction. The only thatched building left in Hutton is 150 Ratten Lane, an eighteenth-century former farmhouse, with many original interior features: when it was built almost all the properties in the township would have been thatched, using local reeds.

19, 20. Most of the farm buildings and cottages in the Grange Lane or Button of Hutton area were rebuilt in red bridck with tiled roofs in the nineteenth century. Some were also altered or upgraded in the 1920s as part of the County Council Smallholdings Scheme.

21. No. 138 Ratten Lane is, with its neighbour No. 140, one of the few early houses remaining in the parish. They are the only small cottages (as contrasted with farmhouses) dating from before the nineteenth century. This photograph shows the cottage in the early twentieth century, long before the renovation and re-roofing which has altered its external appearance. Internally it still preserves many of its original features.

A few Hutton people had possessions which represented another degree of luxury – specialised, often very valuable, small items. Thus John Harrison (1623) had books worth 6s. 0d. (30p); the inventory of Joan or Jennet Marton (1609) includes two silver spoons, a ring and a silver pin (or brooch), together worth 13s. 4d. (62p); and Peter Rawsthorne (1638) had books valued at £1, a set of half a dozen silver spoons worth £1 14s. (£1.70), and a 'fowling piece' (15s., or 75p), the latter giving us a vivid image of the squire going shooting on the marshes, something which Lawrence Rawstorne, nearly 200 years later, would have relished. We are not usually told the titles of the books, although the only book owned by Dorothy Rawsthorne (died 1668) was, predictably enough for a Protestant lady, a *Book of Common Prayer* which was worth 1s. 6d., or 7p. Historians use these fragments of evidence as one partial indicator of the extent of literacy.

The terminology of wills may also give an insight into the public face of religious belief and piety. As is the case elsewhere, seventeenth-century wills from Hutton include a religious preamble, the testament, which expresses hopes about the destiny of the soul. When George Maire, blacksmith of Hutton, made his will in December 1630 he gave his body 'to Christian burial at our parish church of Penwortham where my friends shall think most convenient' (in other words, for him there was no family plot or burying place established by custom). A request for burial at the parish church was frequently included in wills at this period – James Jenkinson, yeoman (1638) included a similar statement in his will, and also made provision for the vicar, Mr Hodson, to make a sermon at his burial. However, it is apparent that although Jenkinson wished to be buried at Penwortham he, like most other Hutton people, actually worshipped at the nearby chapel at Longton, for he provided for a sermon to be said there as well and gave £1 for the purchase of a valuable and expensive book, *I kneel and hard dine*, to be used at Longton chapel. The reason for the apparent discrepancy between the place of his regular attendance at services and the chosen place of his burial is that Longton chapel did not have a graveyard and so no burials took place there.[30] An excellent example of a lengthy and detailed religious testament is given by Robert Mayre (1673):

> I commend my soul into the Merciful hands and heavenly protection of almighty God my Creator, assuredly trusting and unfeignedly believing that in by and through the merits of my God in Jesus Christ, after this transitory life here on earth is ended, my body and soul shall one day again be reunited to live with God in his heavenly kingdom, and be partaker of those incomprehensible joys prepared for his elect and chosen flock for ever, and my body I commit to the earth whereof it was made, and to which again it must return.

Such sentiments are found very widely in wills of this date, but here the reference to the 'elect and chosen flock' might be interpreted as evidence of a puritan or 'low church' inclination, since such terminology would be unusual in a middle-of-the-road Church of England context and would be virtually impossible in a Catholic will. A more Anglican form of phrasing is given in the will of Thomas Maire (1675), who commends his soul 'into the hands of Almighty God my maker hoping that through the meritorious death and passion of Jesus Christ my only

Saviour and Redeemer to Receive free pardon and remission of all my sins'. The precise nature of the personal faith of such individuals will forever be unknown to us, but these more public expressions do reinforce the view that people placed a high importance not only upon religion itself but also upon the proper procedures to be observed when the end was nigh.

In their lifetimes, though, money loomed large in their thinking just as it does for most people today. While the poor struggled to make ends meet or to secure a few pence a week from the township, others higher up the social scale dealt with much larger sums, generating surpluses to be used for investment or needing loans to finance comfortable lifestyles or large expenditure. When people died and inventories were made, such activities appear because these assets, lent, borrowed or accumulated, could represent a substantial part of the 'worldly goods' of the deceased. In the seventeenth century there was no banking system, no safe place to deposit valuables, no formal financial mechanism for credit and loan-giving, and all transactions were still in cash or kind. People might thus keep considerable sums of money in their houses, which was not only a security risk but also meant that the money did not 'work' for them.

For example, Jennet Marton (1609) had a total of £16 15s. in gold and silver in the house when she died – the modern equivalent of this might be something like £8,500. The cash sums are, however, comparatively modest in comparison with the scale of money-lending which in Hutton, as in any other community, was an essential financial mechanism. It was officially subject to disapproval, a hangover from the medieval condemnation of usury, but in reality lending-out by private individuals was scarcely less crucial to the domestic and business economy than lending by banks and building societies is today. Sometimes the sums involved are astonishing, given that the lender was a private individual, and they were often acting as unofficial bankers to dozens of different people. Before Roger Bamber of Hutton died in May 1666 he compiled a list of his debtors, naming fifteen men to whom he had lent money: eight of these were from Hutton, including James Mayer, alehouse keeper, but others were from Preston, Middleforth, Penwortham, Howick and Walton-le-Dale, suggesting that Roger was known locally as a man with spare cash and a willingness to lend. The most curious entry in the list is that for William Robinson of Longton, against whose name is noted 'oweth me for gauld when he was constable last time'. A *gauld* is a rate or levy, and it would seem either that Roger Bamber was himself overcharged on his rate bill or, perhaps more likely, that he lent the constable of Longton some money in advance to cover the anticipated receipts from a rate.

Robert Mayre (1673) had an estate valued at £398 and was probably the wealthiest inhabitant of Hutton, yet of his estate no less than £269 was in the form of secured loans made to local people, and another £13 in unsecured loans. No less than 71% of his assets had thus been used for investment purposes, for these loans would accrue interest repayments and thereby give Robert a double benefit: money lent out was not at risk from theft and robbery (it would otherwise have been stored, vulnerably, as cash) and a regular investment income was created. In modern terms, Robert had lent a total of about £140,000. Henry Mayer was a husbandman or small farmer but on his death in 1641 he was owed £132 'by bills' (i.e., with a signed legal document to confirm the transaction), about £67,000 in today's values. The borrowers were not usually ordinary folk, though some creditors would provide small sums on short-term loan. Any larger loan to the humble was unlikely simply because no security could be offered by those at the bottom levels of society. Instead, many who took loans were farmers needing money to fund agricultural improvement or, more urgently, to tide them over shortfalls in harvests or sales. Jennet Marton (died 1609) had possessions, including the gold and silver referred to earlier, worth £68 13s. 4d. (£68.67), but she was owed another £60 15s. 8d. by a total of 28 individuals to whom she had lent sums ranging from 10s. 0d. to £8 16s., most of these being 'respectable' local people whose security was good. Other borrowers might even be the local gentry. John Stirkliffe died in 1632 and among the five people to whom he had lent money 'by bond' was Mistress Hesketh of Rufford, who had borrowed 14s. (70p). Dorothy Rawstorne, the squire's widow, died in 1662 with £8 3s. of gold and silver in the house, but owing £4 2s. to other people.

14. *Agriculture and Other Trades in the Seventeenth and Eighteenth Centuries*

Most people in Hutton were involved in some way with agriculture, and the evidence for this activity provided by wills and inventories is of special interest. Keeping an animal or two and tilling a small area of land was an essential element in the family economy of all but the landless labourers. Even those whose main occupation was not directly connected with agriculture might aspire to a smallholding. Thus George Maire, described as a blacksmith in his will of 1630, was also a prosperous small farmer, with cattle, horses and sheep valued at £25 4s. and corn and hay worth £28, sums which far outweighed the worth of his blacksmith's tools and stock in trade. George also had property: he left to his son John 'the tenement and several cottages within the lordship of Hutton [now] in my occupation', and refers to his old barn, smithy and his lands in the croft. Inventories do not always specify the numbers of animals which people owned, but when they do we can obtain some impression of the scale of their farming activities, and it is apparent that in the seventeenth century sheep-farming was relatively much more important than it was to be in the nineteenth and twentieth centuries, when dairying came to predominate in this part of the Lancashire plain. Thus John Harrison (1623) had twelve sheep, compared with five milk cows and a calf, and Jennet Marton in 1609 had a very large flock of 49 sheep and hogs (older male sheep) but only five cows. While this was exceptional, most farmers had at least some sheep, and few large herds of cows are recorded in seventeenth-century documents: Dorothy Rawsthorne had twelve cattle, 27 sheep and 16 lambs on her farm in 1662, but the largest herd, not unexpectedly, was probably that of Peter Rawsthorne, whose cattle were valued at £40 in 1638, meaning perhaps twenty or more animals – but even he had about thirty sheep as well.

Mixed farming was the rule, since agricultural specialisation was not yet significant. All communities produced a wide range of food and other commodities for domestic consumption, as well as surpluses for commercial sale in the markets, so a combination of arable and pastoral farming was essential. Hutton had plentiful pasture and rough grazing

22. The lands around the Ribble, from the map of Lancashire published by Christopher Saxton in 1577. The local places named are either the residence of a gentleman (as in the cases of Bank Hall and Walton Hall) or a town or village with a church of chapel. Hutton is not shown – it had no chapel, and the Rawstornes were absentee landowners living elsewhere – but its two main landscape features (the river with its border of sands and marshes, and the great expanse of moss stretching over to Leyland) are clearly indicated.

but the arable element in local agriculture was important even in the late eighteenth century. Ploughs are usually mentioned in inventories, such as that of John Harrison (1632) with his 'husbandry goods as ploughs wheels carts and horse gear', or Peter Rawsthorne, the squire's relative, who in 1638 had 'carts, wheels, ploughs, harrows, horsegear, with odd pieces of cloven and other timber' together worth ten guineas (£10.50). The crops which were grown were relatively few: Robert Mayre (1673) had oats, barley and beans 'upon the ground' (i.e. sown and growing – he died in May) as well as unthreshed wheat in the barn

and barley and beans in the garner, or store, while inside the house
oatmeal worth £1 was kept in the ark, or great chest. Most smaller
farmers probably grew only oats for human consumption (for oatmeal
was the staple food of all poor people and many wealthier ones as well)
and grass for animal fodder, a pattern which is characteristic of seventeenth-century Lancashire. Some also grew wheat and beans, and a few
had peas as a growing crop or stored. Beans, the small coarse ancestors

23. Bill Jackson and his father, after milking at Cockerton Farm in Grange Lane in 1939.
Traditional agricultural practices survived until the time of the Second World War, but
thereafter change was very rapid and many old ways which had gone on for many centuries
ended within a decade.

of broad beans, could be simmered in stews and pottages, or ground into flour which made a thick porridge or eked out bread flour. John Stirkliffe left a 'butt [barrel] of beans' each to widow Barnes and widow Taylor on his death in 1632. There are occasional references, too, to apples and pears, while in deeds and other documents concerning lands orchards are frequently indicated: John Stirkliffe left to Thomas Taylor, son of the widow, 'the young calf that goeth in the orchard'.

Hutton, in common with most of the county, was a cheese and butter-making area in the seventeenth and eighteenth centuries. Salt butter, preserved for long-term use in earthenware butter-mugs, is recorded in some Hutton inventories: Jennet Marton, for example, had three mugs of butter worth 15s. 0d. (75p) in 1609, a mug usually holding 21lb of butter. Dry salt and brine were worked into the butter until it would absorb no more, and then the mug was capped with a wooden disc and sealed with wax or string. The making of butter is implied by Dorothy Rawsthorne's inventory, which included 'butter prints', the decorated wooden bats with which blocks of fresh butter were shaped and marked. Cheese-presses also appear in inventories from the township, as well as whole cheeses stored for future use, and cheese-making was a regular element in the farming year locally until very recent times. The 1915 sale catalogues for the Rawstorne estate, for example, describe Schoolhouse Farm as 'a freehold dairy and cheesemaking farm' with a 'large cheese room'.[74]

As noted above, sheep were important in the economy until the early eighteenth century and their presence is associated with the plentiful evidence for textile production in the township. Today it is unlikely that Hutton would be associated with industry, but for many households here, even as late as the mid-nineteenth century, cloth-weaving was either the main livelihood or a vital supplement to farming. Most seventeenth-century inventories from the township include references to spinning wheels, making it certain that yarn was being produced locally. These were the so-called 'great wheels', which were relatively unsophisticated and were hand-wound (that is, without a foot-treadle).[75] Wool of course came from the sheep which grazed on the marshes with the cattle, but local people also made linen and canvas yarn, the former from flax and the latter from hemp, both of which grew well in the damp conditions locally and were particularly suited to the moss edges and wet streamsides. After harvesting the plants were gathered into large bundles and *retted*

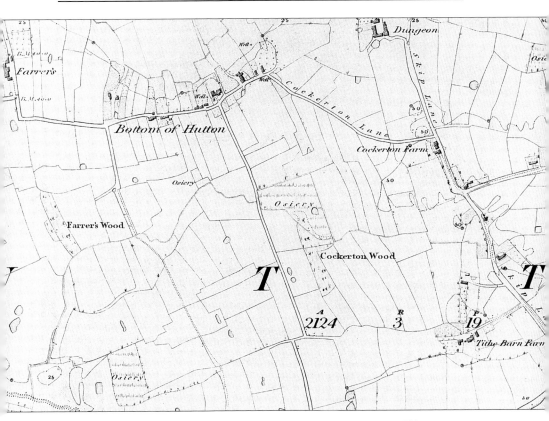

24. Bottom of Hutton in 1845, from the 6-inch to 1-mile Ordnance Survey map. This area
was the old focus of settlement and agricultural activity and today it is the least altered and
most rural part of the parish. The large farms along Grange Lane and Skip Lane were the
successors of the estates which had been held by Cockersand Abbey in the Middle Ages.
Note the osieries, where willows were grown for the local basket-making trade.

in ponds or artificial pits. Retting involved submerging the bundles until
the outer layers of the stalk rotted, producing at a filthy, smelly slime
which was washed away in running water. The strong fibres from the
centre of the stem were then left, and after further treatment could be
spun to make flaxen or hempen yarn.

In 1609 Jennet Marton had in the house seventeen slippings of linen
yarn and sixteen slippings of canvas yarn, worth in total £1 10s. (£1.50
– about £750 in today's values, and she also owned unspun wool
worth 12s.: a slipping was a large hank of yarn, of variable length, which
had been prepared ready for the weaving stage. The quantities of yarn
involved were substantial – lengths are not given but the valuations
indicate that the scale of the spinning industry here was equivalent to

that of south Lancashire, which is better documented. In 1636 John Martin had wool and yarn worth 50s, while in 1662 the lady of the manor, Dorothy Rawsthorne, had flaxen yarn valued at £1 5s., another lot of flaxen yarn, and 81lb of unspun wool worth £1 16s. In total her yarn and unspun wool was worth about £4, which is perhaps £2,000 in today's terms. Once spun, the yarn was bleached, either by being put in the sun, often laid on the grass which gives a natural bleaching effect, or by soaking in various disagreeable solutions of urine and wood ashes: John Stirkliffe in 1632 had 'flaxen and canvas yarn bleached' worth 57s. It was then ready for weaving, but whether this stage was undertaken in Hutton in the seventeenth century is not clear, for none of the inventories searched makes any reference to looms. While this is not conclusive, it does suggest that the yarn might have been taken away to be made into cloth elsewhere. Certainly, the inventory of Robert Maire in 1673 includes not only 'yarn of all sorts' which was in the house, but also 'yarn at the websters [weaver's]', which indicates that, although he was a very prosperous yeoman, his household did not have the comparatively large and costly equipment necessary for weaving. Similarly Dorothy Rawsthorne, also comfortably off, sent her yarn away – her inventory includes 'flaxen yarn in the house and white yarn and cloths at the making'.

However, by the second quarter of the eighteenth century a sizeable domestic weaving industry had arisen in this area, a trend observable elsewhere on the Lancashire plain and perhaps associated with the rapid population increase by then affecting the whole county. Some of the clearest evidence for this apparently new trade comes from the Penwortham parish registers. Although the registers themselves were destroyed by fire in 1858 an annual copy, the bishop's transcript, was made and sent to the diocesan offices in Chester. These transcripts show that between 1724 and 1731 the occupation of the father was recorded in the baptism entries of local children, and from this we can ascertain that eight young men from Hutton, heads of households, were listed either as 'weaver' or 'lin-weaver' during this seven-year period. That may not seem many but, given that the total number of families in Hutton was no more than eighty and perhaps significantly fewer, it is apparent that by the mid-1720s weaving had become an important secondary trade in the township. It is also relevant that the fathers were usually described as linen-weavers, since other evidence suggests that sheep-rearing was of diminishing importance on the Lancashire plain by the middle of the eighteenth century, while flax-growing retained its place in the farming economy. The gradual expansion of the cotton industry is connected with this trend, since fustians, a cotton and linen mixture, became very popular in the later seventeenth century.[76]

15. *Managing the Marsh*

As we have already seen, Hutton's landscape was divisible into four roughly parallel belts of different land uses: the marshes, the enclosed farmlands, the open moor and the mosses. The salt marshes were a very important element in the overall agricultural economy of the township, valuable for the rich grazing which they provided and also significant because they protected and shielded the enclosed farmlands from encroachment by the sea. The marshes were the property of the manor of Hutton, and hence of the Rawstorne family throughout the period from the Reformation to the 1920s, but they were exploited collectively, as many manorial tenants had rights of grazing and also responsibilities to provide labour and materials for the upkeep of the marsh. From at least the middle of the sixteenth century the gradual reclamation of the marshes had been a goal of successive lords and stewards, for as the marsh dried out and was less subject to tidal inundation it eventually became excellent pasture, but progress was always slow and unsure, and frequently reversed by flooding of salt water and incursions from the sea.[77]

A very detailed picture of the way in which the marsh was managed in its heyday can be obtained from the financial accounts kept by the manorial steward and entitled 'Hutton Marsh Callings'.[78] They survive from 1712 to 1732 and are extremely detailed, with an annual recitation of all expenditure and listing of all the rents which were paid to the manor for grazing rights. As elsewhere on the shores of the Ribble, the marshland grazing was divided into 'gates', which were allocations of shares in the grazing. The total number of beasts which could be supported in each season was calculated, and then that figure was divided in proportion to the number of gates which each individual owner or

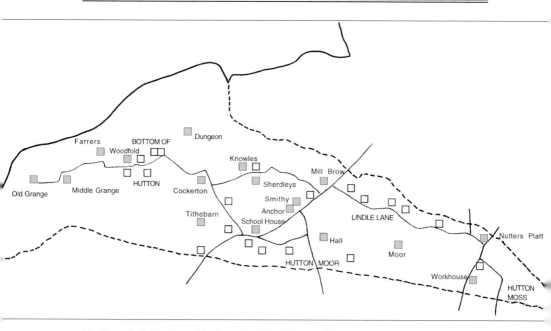

25. Farms in Hutton township, from the 1845 Ordnance Survey map.

tenant held. The arithmetic was exceedingly complicated, for in 1712 there were 113⅞ marsh gates in Hutton, which were held by nineteen different individuals in varying numbers. The great majority, 93¾ gates, were owned by William Rawstorne, the squire, while the other eighteen men shared the remaining 20⅛ marsh gates – some had as little as ⅑ of a gate. The peculiar proportions of gates, and the eccentric overall total, are the result of two processes first, the frequent subdivision of allocations as portions or shares were sold off or divided between heirs, and second, the addition of extra fractions of gates as the regulation and improvement of the marsh continued and it was deemed to be capable of supporting more animals. The list below shows the complete allocation in 1712 and highlights the way in which rights to Hutton grazings had, by purchase or hereditary descent, been acquired by individuals who lived in some cases miles from the township. In such cases the rights were often sub-let to local people, who otherwise would not benefit from a share in the marsh grazing, and as long as the manorial steward knew of this practice, and the numbers of beasts did not exceed the allocation for each gate, the leasing of rights was permitted.

Marshgates and rents paid for them, 1712

Thomas Ashurst of Ashurst	⅑ of a gate	£00–00–05
Thomas Miller of Hutton	⅑	£00–00–05
Widow Simson alias Parke	⅙	£00–00–07½
Robert Southworth of Hutton	¼	£00–00–11½
Robert Wilding of Hutton	¼	£00–00–11½
John Forshaw of Tarleton	⅓	£00–01–03
Mr Thomas Walton of Howick	⅑	£00–00–05
Mr Thomas Whalley of Preston	⅖	£00–01–06
Nathan Haworth of Fazakerley	⅖	£00–01–06
Hugh Waring of Hutton	1	£00–03–09½
Thomas Hesketh of Rufford, esq.	1	£00–03–09½
William Marton of Hutton	1¼	£00–04–08¾
Mr Knott of Walton	1⅖	£00–04–08¾
Mr Sherdley of Poulton	1½	£00–05–08¼
Mr Fleetwood of Banks, esq.	4	£00–15–02
Henry Fleetwood of Penwortham esq.	3¼	£00–12–03¾
Mr Loxham of Longton	4¼	£00–16–01¼
William Rawstorne esq.	93¾	£17–15–05¼
Totals	113⅞	£21–11–11¾

The accounts unfortunately do not state, for any year, the actual numbers of cattle or sheep which were grazed, and therefore we cannot know the value of each gate or fraction of a gate in terms of the beasts which it represented, but the grazing was a very valuable commodity and was highly prized. The complexity of the allocations, and the care taken to ensure that the system was observed, make this plain. Had it not been valuable, the marsh grazing would not have warranted such elaborate management. We do know how many manorial tenants were allowed to rent shares of the lord's marshgates, for a list of 1720 gives the names of all sixty individuals who held tenancies from the manor. Of these 26 are described as having 'no common' – that is, no grazing on the marsh – and the other 34 have portions of manorial marshgates in rough proportion to the area of land which they farmed. The list is given as an appendix to this book.

Statements of the legal title to the marshgates can be found in manorial leases and other documents relating to tenancies. A good instance is provided by a lease of 13 May 1777, which includes among the lands and assets 'all that one Beastgate or herbage and pasturage for one Cow or other full grown horned Cattle or instead and Lieu thereof for the usual and accustomed Number of Sheep or other Cattle in proportion thereto and also half another Beastgate and all other Right and priviledge of Common … to be had yearly for ever in and upon the stinted [79] pasture Marsh or Common called Hutton Marsh'. A beastgate was thus the right to graze a full-grown cow, or other animals according to a scale of equivalents. A collection of beastgates, or rights to graze individual beasts, would make up a marshgate, a larger and defined share of the total grazing. A tenant or a marshgate owner might, as the list above indicates, have fractions or multiples of a marshgate. It was a sophisticated and complex system, arithmetically challenging and subtly adapted to the needs of the community and (a vital consideration) to ensure careful husbanding and conservation of the vegetation of the marsh, to prevent overgrazing.

Physically the marshgates did not exist on the ground, for there were no fences, walls or hedges on the marsh proper and the animals were free to roam at will across it. Hutton Marsh, like the adjacent marshes of Howick, Penwortham and Longton, consisted of a tract of open saltmarsh, covered with cropped wiry turf and salt-tolerant plants, and dissected by an intricate network of winding channels and steep-sided gulleys. The land was above the normal tidal limit, so that for much of the year it was accessible for grazing, but was completely covered at the higher tides, especially those of the spring and autumn equinoxes. For this reason, as well as for the better preservation of the turf, grazing was permitted in the summer months only, between the equinoxial flooding. Along the inner edge of the marsh was a network of embankments or cops, made of earth but reinforced with piles, stone revetments and brushwood barriers. These banks protected the marshland which had been reclaimed and converted to permanent pasture, since the 'new lands' were below highest tide levels and vulnerable to flooding. Mill Brook and Longton Brook drained out across the marsh and there were tide sluices at their inner mouths, to prevent the sea reaching up their shallow valleys.

The seasonal nature of the grazing, and the difficulty of undertaking work in winter, early spring or early autumn, meant that much of the annual maintenance work, especially the reinforcing and strengthening of the banks, took place in spring and mid-autumn, which were also times when farm work was limited so that labour could be spared for marsh projects. The work undertaken on the marsh including making gates and wooden rail fences which divided the grazing lands from the enclosed farmland; constructing brushwood hurdles which were used to reinforce and strengthen the banking; and maintaining the streamsides, sluices and channels to prevent erosion and flooding. The work used very large quantities of wood, some of it obtained locally at Blashaw Wood in Penwortham, but much of it felled seasonally from the magnificent and beautiful hanging woods which clothed (as they still do) the meanders of the Ribble at Osbaldeston, Alston and Elston below Ribchester. Other timber, particularly the alders which grew on the riverside, came from Hothersall, and some from Barton north of Preston. The accounts include numerous entries referring to the felling, shifting, carting and storage of timber and brushwood. Particularly interesting are the accounts for 1731 and 1732, when the timber was felled in Tunbrook, the valley which runs down from Grimsargh to the river at Red Scar. John Comeleach was paid for seven and a half days' rafting, and other men for taking up the wood from the river, while fishermen were compensated for their assistance in the latter task and for damage to nets and fishing stakes. Here we have a fascinating insight into an otherwise unrecorded use of the river – rafts of timber were floated down from the Alston and Samlesbury area and intercepted either at the boathouse in Penwortham, close to the old Penwortham Bridge, for transport overland to Hutton, or allowed to continue on the ebb tide to the Hutton shore where they were landed by the fishermen. The costs of all these activities was shared out among the marsh tenants in proportion to their holdings of marshgates, so that in 1713, for example, each marshgate was charged 4s. 10¾d. and in 1719 3s. 7d.

Although the upkeep of the marsh defences was a major part of the task, the manor and its leading tenants were also actively concerned with reclaiming sections of the marsh, enclosing them by new embankments and creating additional fields. We can reconstruct the progress of one such venture in the decade up to 1722, as a new field was created – it is relatively unusual to be able to date such a project so precisely, and to see in such detail the way in which the work was carried out. In the early spring, after the highest tides, piles were driven into the marsh, using alder wood which rots only very slowly: in 1713, 600 alderwood piles were brought from Hothersall and in the following year a further 700. The next stage was to surround the piles with embankments of earth and sand, probably using material thrown up by the digging of drainage ditches alongside the intended field. In 1722 the field was ready and hedges were planted along its borders, with four bunches of quicksets (probably hawthorn), 300 alder saplings, and 60 of ash. There was substantial expenditure on ditching work, on 'evening' – that is, levelling

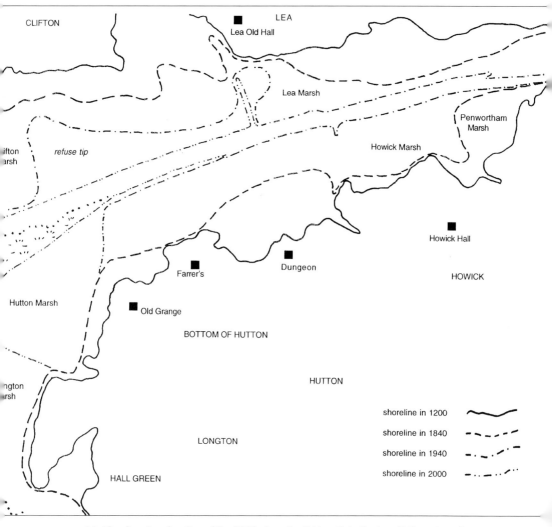

26. The changing shoreline of the Ribble from the thirteenth to the twentieth century. Over the past eight hundred years, and especially since the eighteenth century, the estuary of the Ribble has disappeared as a result of reclamation, embanking and drainage works, which have produced thousands of acres of new farmland. The gradual retreat of the sea, and the turning of the salt marsh into regular agricultural land, has added large areas of new ground to parishes such as Hutton.

the ground – and on mowing the rushes which had grown in the damp ground. Finally, as the land dried out, it was ploughed and raked and after several years' of hard labour and painstaking endeavour a new field had been created from the marsh. Records of such enclosure on the inner edge of the marsh may also be identified among the leases and tenancy agreements which were made by the Rawstornes as lords of the manor. In 1748, for example, a lease between Lawrence Rawstorne and Thomas Harrison refers to a tiny portion of marsh, 28 perches in area, which legally belonged with other lands in Hutton and was 'formerly apportioned and allotted thereto according to Divisions made … by Consent and Agreement of the Lords and Charterers of the said Marsh'.[80]

16. *The Fisheries*

Beyond the marshes were the sands and the estuary. The relationship between the land and sea was an ever-present theme in these coastal communities, where the reclamation and improvement of the marshes was constantly challenged by the tides and salt water. Today it is not obvious that Hutton was a truly coastal township, because the reclamation of the Ribble marshes and sands has progressed to the point where the tidal channel is relatively remote and narrow, and the open water is well down the river, but until the nineteenth century the tides regularly lapped at the foot of Old Grange and Bottom of Hutton. As a coastal community Hutton had its fishermen, who worked the sands and chan-nels of the river and knew it intimately. They were a small and self-contained group, sharing their working lives with other fishermen from Howick, Longton and Becconsall as they worked out in the estuary. They appear in the historical record only infrequently, although we have seen how there are some references to nets and fisheries in the thirteenth century and in the 1720s and 1730s they were mentioned in the accounts for managing the marsh. There survives a list of 'The names of the fyshers att huton water' which was compiled in 1621: Rafe Wilding, son of Thomas; John Philipson, son of Richard; John Marshaw; Henry Wilding, son of Richard; and Thomas Wilding, son of Thomas.[81]

The fisheries were owned by the lords of the manor, the Rawstorne family, and were leased out to the fishermen for an annual rent. The boundaries were carefully guarded: in 1758 an agreement was signed between Sir Henry Houghton of Hoghton Tower, the owner of the fisheries of Lea on the opposite side of the river, William Farington of Worden, who was the lessee of the Lea fisheries, and Lawrence Rawstorne, confirming that the boundary of the two fisheries lay in the middle of the deep water channel of the river.[82] A rare glimpse into the methods of the local fishermen is found in some notes [83] made in about 1830 as evidence during a dispute over fishing rights. The notes include details of the rental payments: the Rawstornes leased the fisheries to James Singleton, for a rent of £10 10s. (ten guineas) per annum, a sum which is noted in 1803 and continued to the late 1820s, and had probably been unaltered for many decades. Singleton in turn sub-let the fishing to the local men who, giving evidence, testified as to their methods.

William Knowles, aged 65 (and thus born about 1765), had lived in Hutton all his life. He said that he never 'joined in the fishery' – that is, paid a rent for fishing rights – but he often worked with those who had. Fifty years previously, in the early 1780s, three men, William Moss, Robert Franklin and William Harrison, fished the Hutton Sands using baulks of timber, a method which was still employed in the 1830s when the document was drawn up. Temporary wooden dams were built across channels on the sands and the outer edges of the marsh, so that at high tide the dams were submerged and the fish came up towards the shore to feed. As the tide ebbed the dams trapped the fish in the channels, where they could be caught with nets. Richard Harrison, the son of William Harrison, also testified. He was 74, so born about 1755, had 'known the Hutton fisheries all my life', and agreed that the baulks were the only method used by the Hutton men. When he was a boy men called Abrams, Blundell and Peter Houghton had been the lessees, then the three named by Knowles.

The most detailed statement was given by William Burscough of Longton, also 74 years old, who had regularly worked the Hutton Sands as an 'assistant' to Moss, Franklin and Harrison. They would he said, 'set 2 or 3 Baulks, the number depended on the channels, the size of the Baulks would depend on the size of them [the channels]'. He recalled that they were usually set for flukes, the small flatfish which are extremely common along the shallow Lancashire coasts and which were the main-stay of the fishing industry from the Crosby shore right up to Morecambe

Bay, but he also claimed, no doubt correctly, that there were never as many baulks in Hutton as in Longton (which had a much larger area of sands). The fishing was thus small in scale, but locally important and – as the Harrisons suggest – often passed on as a trade from father to son. It survived into the late nineteenth century, but was ever-threatened by the diminishing area of the sands themselves. As reclamation proceeded, the fisheries were lost, and this process reached its inevitable conclusion after 1885 when, with the building of Preston Dock and the canalisation of the river, the sands themselves disappeared and with them the last traces of this ancient occupation.

17. *Enclosing the Moor and Reclaiming the Moss*

The moor was a major component of the medieval landscape of Hutton, just as in adjacent townships. Names such as Howick Moor Lane and Moorhey Drive in Penwortham, as well as Moor Lane in Hutton itself, remind us that open grazing land extended through the area in a belt between the mosses to the east and the enclosed farmlands to the west. The disappearance of this open land, and its subdivision into conventional fields which were privately occupied, was not only an important change to the local landscape but also a significant alteration in the way that the community functioned. Once a common asset, available for all the tenants of the manor, the moor was gradually 'privatised' and taken out of communal use. In this the experience of Hutton was entirely typical of that of other communities in north-west England, where by the late eighteenth century the only substantial tracts of common grazing land were the high moorlands of the Pennines. We have little detailed information about the enclosing of the moor in Hutton, because it was a piecemeal business, not planned and implemented as a whole, but we can be sure that it was already under way by the mid-sixteenth century. At that time the population growth and economic expansion evident throughout south Lancashire provided a new impetus for enclosure. The conversion of rough grazing land to improved pasture facilitated more intensive forms of agriculture including stock-rearing and dairying on a

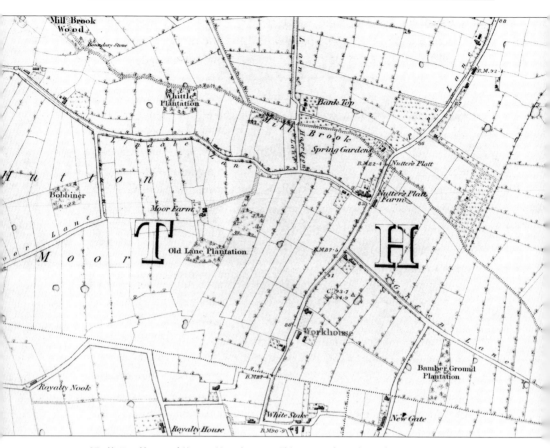

27. Hutton Moor and Hutton Moss in 1845. This extract from the Ordnance Survey 6-inch to 1-mile sheet shows the pattern of small regular fields which resulted from the enclosure of the open moor and moss in the period from the fifteenth to the eighteenth century, together with some of the isolated farms which had been established on the areas which had been brought into more intensive agricultural use. The 1827 workhouse in what is now Pope Lane is also clearly marked.

larger scale. Improved pasture commanded much higher rents than simple grazing rights, and so was potentially lucrative for the lords of the manor, but there was also a need for new farms and smallholdings on the former wastes to feed and accommodate the growing population. In Hutton it is likely that the transfer of ownership from monastic control to the Rawstorne family also accelerated the enclosure of the moor, for the new lords had a more direct and immediate need to raise greater revenues from rents.

The main evidence for piecemeal enclosure comes from the leases to tenants made by the Rawstorne estate in the eighteenth century, which give a picture of small-scale encroachment upon the moor to create new fields. Individually the leases are not always helpful because they rarely indicate the exact date at which enclosure took place. A lease of January 1719, for example, refers to 1½ acres which was part of 'the new enclos'd Common called Hutton Moor' and in 1728 there is reference to 'two acres lately inclosed from the common moor within Hutton'.[84] Such phrases continue throughout the eighteenth century. Thus, in February 1788 a lease concerning land in the vicinity of Lindle Lane and Balmoral Road referred to 'parcels of ground called New Ground or Moor Ground' (that is, land enclosed from the moor) and in the following year another lease from the same area included the phrase 'two acres of land some time since inclosed from the Common or Moor within Hutton'.[85] Occasionally there is a hint of a more precise dating, as in a lease of November 1757 when a Moor Field belonging to, but physically some distance from, a property in Ratten Row is described as 'recently Inclosed', and at least one definite instance can be identified. In September 1737 a lease of land in Saunders Lane includes a reference to fields 'formerly part of Hutton Moor' but also mentions a fine of £17 for improving one acre on the moor', a current payment to the lord for the privilege of taking-in common land.[86]

That some of the moor therefore survived into the middle of the eighteenth century seems likely. A lease of May 1748 includes the provision that the tenant shall enjoy the use of the proportionate number of beastgates on the marsh, and 'the like proportionable part of the Commons or Moors or other Waste Ground in Hutton aforesaid when the same shall be enclosed'. This implies that there were unenclosed common moors at that date[87] but that their final enclosure was anticipated. Similar wording had been more common in the late seventeenth and early eighteenth centuries, but the 1748 example is perhaps the last. It is certain that the common moor had vanished and had parcelled out into privately-occupied fields by the end of the century and that perhaps in the 1760s or 1770s, the last fragments, no longer viable as common grazing, were enclosed for private use. Today all that remains of the moor is a street name – Moor Lane – and the surviving remnants of the fields which replaced it, east of the police headquarters on the north side of New Longton.

As the moor was gradually disappearing, agricultural improvements were reducing the area of Hutton Moss. There, too, no single concerted attempt was made to reclaim and enclose the wetland, but instead a slow process of drainage and making new fields can be identified from leases and other manorial documents. The moss was small in comparison with the vast tracts of wetland in townships such as Longton, Ulnes Walton and Farington, and it was probably relatively straightforward to drain by digging ditches and channels to carry the surplus waters into Wymott Brook and Mill Brook. Some open moss remained in the 1720s – a lease of 1728 refers to 'six acres of moss ground in Wymott in Hutton'[88] – but when William Yates' made his one-inch to one-mile map of Lancashire in 1786 the moss had completely disappeared. Again, the middle years of the eighteenth century seem to have been a crucial time, when the old agricultural patterns and landscapes finally gave way to new forms.

The Rawstornes, as lords of the manor and by far the most important landowners, were instrumental in effecting these changes. They and

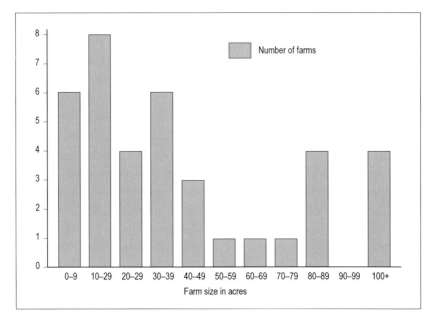

28. Farm sizes in Hutton in 1851 (from the information contained in the census returns of that year). The graph shows that Hutton had a large number of comparatively small farms, especially of between 10 and 40 acres, and several very large estates, but relatively few medium sized properties. This reflects its traditional social structure, observable in records since at least the seventeenth century, whereby a few large farmers dominated a large group of smallholders and (not reflected on this chart) landless labourers.

successive stewards pushed for improvement, including reclamation and enclosure, and by the late eighteenth century the estate as a whole had undergone major development. The value of the Hutton properties increased very considerably after the 1780s, when the township became one of the main contributors to the wealth of the Rawstorne family. In the early years of the nineteenth century Lawrence Rawstorne carried through the extravagant project to rebuild Hutton Hall as a dower house for his mother and unmarried sisters, while at the same time largely rebuilding Penwortham Priory as his own home. The implication was that the Penwortham property was more important, but the figures which Rawstorne calculated to show his income in the year 1814 tell a different story. They are summarised in the table below:

	Gross rent income	*Minus Land Tax*	*Net rent income*
Penwortham	£1,529–11–10	£152–18–00	£1,376–06–00
Howick	£ 341–12–04	£ 34–03–00	£ 307–09–04
Hutton	£4,326–10–09	£432–00–00	£3,893–17–09

He also noted income from other sources: the Rossendale estate rents brought in £587, and those of Preston £212, Farington £714, Parr near St Helens £5, Longton £31, and North Meols £40. He also had income from the tithes which he owned (Hutton, £130 10s., Leyland £216, Longton £216, Penwortham £203, Howick £54) as well as a miscellany of minor profits – shares in the Ribble Navigation Company £17 10s., shares in the Haslingden turnpike £15, and rents from the church pews at Leyland, £5. Overall, therefore, his net income from the estates and associated assets was about £8,000 a year, of which almost exactly one-half was derived from the Hutton properties and the tithes of the township. While Hutton may not have been his chosen place to live, it made by far the greatest contribution to funding a lifestyle which even he noted was beyond his means.[89] Although heavily preoccupied with the building projects and with his leisure pursuits of hunting and shooting, Lawrence Rawstorne was very conscious of the importance of the estate and his diaries make many references to farming activities. He encouraged the creation of small woodlands and belts of trees, for agricultural reasons but also, perhaps more significantly from his perspective, as game cover. Thus, in September 1811 he notes that 'the field at the back of the garden by the Grange was planted March 1808. As was also the ground betwixt the garden at Hutton and Spencer's'. As he rode around his estates, such indicators of farming progress and landscape management must have gladdened his heart.

18. *Hutton in the Nineteenth Century: The Census Evidence*

During the eighteenth century the population of Hutton increased rapidly. Historians continue to debate the causes of population growth at this time, for it was a national trend, but there was probably a general rise in the birth rate and in fertility, perhaps occasioned by factors such as people marrying earlier. Whether death rates were falling is less certain, but it is clear that all over England the population was increasing. Agriculture was still the most important occupation in the township, but the expansion of Lancashire's textile industry was having an impact even in rural areas such as this by the 1720s, as indicated by the evidence from the parish registers quoted earlier. This change, whereby the local economy was diversified and, we may assume, income levels tended to rise so that people were better-off, meant that rural communities such as Hutton could support a larger population. Instead of the surplus being forced off the land and into urban areas, much of the population growth could be absorbed locally. It was in this period, and especially in the half-century before 1830, that many of the weavers' cottages were built in areas such as Hutton to accommodate the expanding population.

The earliest precise figure we have for the population of Hutton is given in the first national census, taken in April 1801, when Hutton township had a population of 462, and 90 families. The extent of handloom weaving is indicated by the accompanying statistics for employment. Of the occupied population, 61 people were 'chiefly employed in agriculture' and 102 in 'trade, manufactures or handicrafts'. No more detailed breakdown is given, so we cannot be sure how many of the latter category were engaged in weaving, but the reasonable presumption is that most were. Hutton had very few retailers, craftsmen or tradesmen, and therefore the great majority were likely to have been in the manufacturing sector, in which handloom-weaving was by far the most important element. Thus, at the start of the nineteenth century Hutton was in appearance a rural and agricultural community, but its economy had been reorientated towards industry. Hutton people wove cloth in their homes, using cotton yarn which by this time probably came from steam or water-powered mills in towns and villages to the east.

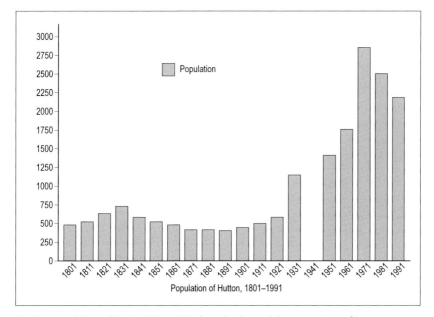

Population of Hutton, 1801–1991

29. The population of Hutton 1801–1991, from the decennial census returns (there was no census in 1941 because of the Second World War). The graph shows very clearly the decline in population in the mid-nineteenth century after several decades of steady growth, and the dramatic effects of suburban house-building in the fifty years from the mid-1920s.

Ten years later, the next census recorded a population of 507, a growth of just under 10% in a decade. That would have been impressive enough, but the population increase between 1811 and 1821 was remarkable – it grew by 21%, to 613, a rate which was sustained during the 1820s, since in 1831 there were 713 people, a further 17% increase. Therefore, between 1801 and 1831 the population of this rural township had increased by 55%, a growth which was made possible almost entirely by the prosperity brought by handloom weaving. In the 1831 census rather more detailed employment figures are given for males over 20 years of age, and these can be summarised as follows: [90]

Total numbers of males 20 years or more	160
Engaged in agriculture	52 (33%)
of whom, farmers or smallholders not employing labourers	17 (11%)
farmers or smallholders employing labourers	12 (8%)
agricultural labourers	23 (14%)
Employed in manufacturing	85 (53%)
Employed in retailing or crafts	8 (5%)
Professionals or capitalists	3 (2%)
Others, including general labourers and servants	12 (8%)

This table demonstrates most effectively how Hutton had become an industrial township, something which now seems scarcely possible given the almost complete absence of industry locally. The figures in fact understate the true position, since many handloom weavers were women and girls and they do not appear in this table. But this remarkable phenomenon did not rest on secure foundations, for everything depended upon the continued viability of handloom weaving. The golden age of the trade had been the years after 1780, when steam-powered spinning mills were turning out vastly increased quantities of yarn, but when steam had not yet been applied to the processes involved in weaving. It was, with hindsight, inevitable that the technological breakthrough of steam-looms would soon come, and when it did the handloom weaving industry would be immediately threatened. That change began in the 1830s, and the population figures for 1841 starkly emphasise the consequent sudden reversal of fortune which was experienced by places such as Hutton. Between 1831 and 1841 the population fell from 713 to 563, by 1851 it had reduced to 500, and in 1861 to 461, less than it had been sixty years before and a decrease of 36% in three decades. There was, in other words, a large-scale exodus from Hutton as people, thrown out of work in the handloom weaving trade, sought new employment and new lives elsewhere.

After 1861 the decline in population continued, although at a slower rate. The lowest recorded population for the township of Hutton was in 1891, when only 374 inhabitants are recorded in the census, far below the 1801 figure and probably about equivalent to the 1720s' figure. These were traumatic years for rural communities on the edges of the Lancashire textile areas – comparable patterns could be shown for many other townships in the area of south Ribble and the west Lancashire plain [91]

– and they effectively contradict the notion that such places were sleepy backwaters, unchanging and unaltering, until the twentieth century. We know little about where the people went, but many ended up in towns such as Preston, Blackburn and Chorley, others moved to the cities, still others overseas to the colonies: when, in 1836, the Mormons made their first-ever mission beyond the United States, they came to Preston, and in the next ten years groups of people from the Longton and Hutton area made the long sea crossing and arduous overland trek to find what they hoped would be a better life in the plains and deserts of Utah.

The 1851 census gives us our first really detailed picture of the inhabitants of Hutton, since for the previous censuses in 1801 to 1841 the returns were either summary totals or have been destroyed. In 1851, for example, birthplaces, precise ages and precise descriptions of occupations are given, each of which is lacking from earlier returns. The employment and occupational data from this census reinforces the conclusion as to the importance of handloom weaving, but also gives us a breakdown of the other crafts and trades within the community. In 1851, even after fifteen years of continuous rapid decline in the trade, handloom weaving still accounted for 90 of the employed population of Hutton – almost one in every five people, and one in every four adults, was a weaver. Particularly striking is the significance of this occupation in terms of female employment. Whereas in towns there was a wide range of casual or formal work for women, this was much less so in rural areas, especially as Lancashire did not have a strong tradition of women in agriculture. The figures for female employment in 1851 are given below:

Domestic service and domestic work		61
domestic work at home	48	
domestic [house] servant	9	
housekeeper	8	
nurse	2	
Weaving		40
of which powerloom 1, and handloom	39	
Agricultural employment		10
Farmers	3	
Agricultural labourers or farmworkers	5	
Cow-tenters	2	
Others		10

Washerwomen	6
Dressmakers	2
Milliner	1
Schoolmistress	1

Most of the women and girls listed as doing 'domestic work at home' were the wives and daughters of householders, and so did not contribute to the family income (which is not to deny the importance of what they did, of course), and thus the significance of weaving as an additional source of money for the household is apparent. So, too, is the very limited range of work otherwise available to women. However, handloom weaving was also a very important occupation for men. There were 51 male weavers, and the census returns show that many Hutton households were entirely dependent upon this trade for their livelihood. In all, 179 people, or 36% of the population, lived in a household where there was at least one handloom weaver, but the following examples show situations where almost everybody was engaged in the trade – the Hesketh family returns suggest that even the apparently wealthier families might rely heavily on this work:

Workhouse Lane [Pope Lane]

Edward COOKE	aged 64	handloom weaver	born Penwortham
Jane, his wife	aged 58	employed in domestic work	born Hutton
Thomas, their son	aged 31	handloom weaver	born Hutton
Anne, their daughter	aged 22	handloom weaver	born Hutton
Nathaniel, their son	aged 18	handloom weaver	born Hutton

The Turnpike Road [Hutton Row]

Mary NORRIS	aged 45	handloom weaver	born Longton
Stephen, her son	aged 24	handloom weaver	born Longton
Ann, her daughter	aged 22	handloom weaver	born Longton
William, her son	aged 20	agricultural labourer	born Longton
Jane, her daughter	aged 16	handloom weaver	born Longton
Margaret, her daughter	aged 14	employed at home	born Longton
Catherine, her daughter	aged 11	cow-tenter	born Longton
Mally, her daughter	aged 8		born Longton
Robert, her son	aged 4		born Longton
Ellen, her daughter	aged 2		born Longton
Thomas, her son	6 months		born Longton

Bottom of Hutton

John HESKETH	aged 79	farmer of 75 acres	born Penwortham
Ellen, his wife	aged 76	handloom weaver	born Penwortham
Ellen, their daughter	aged 36	handloom weaver	born Hutton
Margaret, their daughter	aged 34	handloom weaver	born Hutton
Isabella, their daughter	aged 27	handloom weaver	born Hutton
Henry, their grandson	aged 15	agricultural labourer	born Hutton
Joseph SINGLETON, lodger	aged 26	gamekeeper	born Goosnargh

Although virtually every rural community had its crafts and service trades, places such as Hutton had only a basic range of such occupations and it did not even, for example, have a resident blacksmith at that time, although a smithy adjacent to the *Anchor* is recorded in the later nineteenth century. The proximity of Longton, which although not a market town had some of the character of one as a local shopping and social centre, meant that these service trades and local crafts were within easy reach. The 1851 census lists the following for Hutton, in each case with only one person employed in that trade unless otherwise stated:

publican	sawyer	basket-maker
wheelwright	thatcher	brick and tile makers (2)
gardener	glazier	tailor
cordwainer		

NB: a cordwainer was a shoemaker; the brick and tile makers presumably worked at the brickyards in Longton, where the Brickcroft is today

The one basket-maker is of some interest, for we know that basket-making was a trade of some importance in the townships further to the south, around the edges of the mosses in places such as Mawdesley, Croston and Rufford. In Hutton itself the six-inch to one-mile map published in 1845 shows, in the area of Bottom of Hutton and Liverpool Road, a number of osieries, where the willows or osiers were grown to supply the raw material for the basket-making trade. They are all in wet hollows, the former small patches of moss which had not been drained but were now being exploited for this important local resource. The trade disappeared from the Hutton area by the later nineteenth century, although it survived at Mawdesley until the late 1950s, but it was an ancient craft – among the probate inventories of the seventeenth century is that of Robert Mayre (1673) whose possessions included 'withing wood at the back of the barn', this being withies, or osiers.

Another aspect of employment which is of special interest to historians

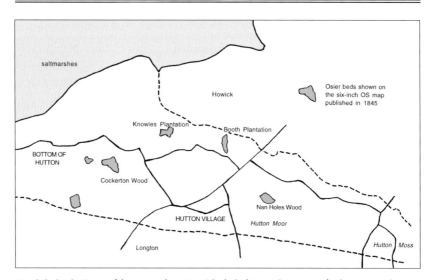

30. Osieries in Hutton (shown on the 1845 6-inch Ordnance Survey map): these were the places where the osiers, or willows, were grown to provide the long flexible twigs used in the basket-making trade, which had considerable local importance until the late nineteenth century.

and to those investigating the past of communities in Lancashire is child labour. We are familiar with images of children working in mills and coal mines, but these were not the only places where it was found. In Hutton in 1851 there were 208 children aged 15 years or under, and of these 44 were working. Their employment is summarised in the following table:

	Boys	Girls
Handloom weaving	5	5
Domestic employment	1	11
Nurse		1
Agricultural labourers	13	3
Cow tenters	1	2
Dressmaker		1
Errand boy	1	

The youngest children listed as 'employed' were both eight years old – a girl who was a cow-tenter and the errand boy. The census figures suggest that boys from labouring families might start work at the age of ten or eleven, if they were destined to be agricultural workers, and that girls started 'domestic work', either at home or going out to service, a year or so later. Hutton children were relatively fortunate in that here, even before the 1870 Education Act which introduced compulsory elementary schooling, there were educational opportunities. In 1851 there were 75 'scholars' aged fifteen or less, amounting to 37% of the total number of children, but in the crucial period from 6 to 10 years old, when elementary schooling was most likely to be acquired, only seven children were working and another ten (four boys and six girls) were receiving no education – in other words, most children in Hutton by the early years of Victoria's reign were being given at least a rudimentary form of schooling. Howick School was just over the township boundary, but it was of special benefit to the children of Hutton, most of whom attended for two or three years and some of whom went on to the grammar school itself.

The other information from the 1851 census which is of particular interest is that concerning birthplaces. The study of migration patterns and population movement in Victorian England would scarcely be possible without such data. Even for a small community such as Hutton the information is very revealing, emphasising as it does that rural life was far from static and that, contrary to the popular belief, people in fact moved very often and to stay in one place for a lifetime was actually relatively unusual. However, the 1851 census for Hutton, while confirming that people were mobile, also highlights another aspect, namely, that rural communities such as this were almost untouched by the greatest population movement experienced by nineteenth-century Lancashire – the Irish influx which was already under way by 1800 and swelled to a flood during the mid-1840s as a result of the Famine. In 1851, when about 20% of the population of Liverpool was Irish-born, there was only one such person in Hutton. Places such as Hutton had no attractions to the Irish and offered them no opportunities or enticements beyond that of seasonal agricultural work. Indeed, as we have seen, by 1851 Hutton itself was a source of emigrants, who were leaving the rural areas not so much because of agricultural problems but because of the collapse of weaving.

The statistics for 1851 instead point to a pattern of large-scale but short-distance movement which is very similar to that identified in other rural areas at this time. Only 42% of the population of Hutton in 1851 was born in the township – thus, well over half the people of Hutton came from elsewhere. This is long before the influx of newcomers which resulted, in the twentieth century, from Hutton's growth as a residential

HUTTON TOWNSHIP
Private residents and farmers in 1851

Breakall, Richard (victualler, *Blue Anchor*)
Burnett, Thomas (registrar of births and deaths for Longton district)
Grammar School:
Rev. W. Harrison, M.A., head master;
Thomas Burnett, and Thomas

Hindle, assistant masters;
Catherine Nailer, mistress
Hunt, Mrs Sarah (Brown cottage)
Rawsthorne, Rev. Robert Atherton (incumbent of Penwortham, Hutton hall)
Smalley, Thomas (assistant overseer)

Farmers

Almond, James
Alty, Thomas (Dungeon Farm)
Ball, Oliver (Old grange)
Blundall, James (Middle grange)
Blundall, Richard (Lindal lane)
Carr, Isabella
Clegg, William
Hesketh, John
Hindle, Thomas
Hindle, Ralph
Johnson, John
Knowles, Thomas
Knowles, John
Linaker, John (Farrers farm)
Mayor, John
Mayor, William
Moss, Thomas
Moss, Rhomas (Rotton Row)

Moss, William (Skip lane)
Norris, Richard (Mill brow farm)
Rainsforth, James
Robinson & Wilson
Sergeant, Matthew
Sergeant, Richard
Singleton, Ezekiel (Lindal lane)
Slater, William senior (Back lane)
Slater, William junior (Skip lane)
Slater, Ellen
Smalley, Martha
Smith, William
Stephenson, John
Sutton, Richard (Moor farm)
Taylor, Matthew (Nutter's plat)
Whittle, Ellen (Workhouse farm)
Worsley, William

Adapted from Mannex & Co., *History and Directory of the Borough of Preston and Seven Miles Round with the Town and Parish of Chorley* (1851)

commuter settlement, indicating that the population has always been 'on the move'. Many of the incomers, however, had come only a short distance, as the following table suggests:

Birthplaces of Hutton residents in 1851

Birthplace	Number	Percentage of total
Hutton	210	42%
Longton	57	11%
North Meols	44	9%
Penwortham	36	7%
Much and Little Hoole	25	5%
Bretherton	16	

Leyland	13
Preston	9
Farington	7
Croston	6
Tarleton	6
Walton le Dale	5
Lytham	5
Howick	4
Other places in Lancashire	49
Rest of England	6
Ireland and overseas	2

Thus, just over 20% of the population came from the immediately adjoining townships (Longton, Penwortham, Farington and Howick) and adding the Hutton-born residents to this total gives an overall figure of 314 born within the parish of Penwortham, or 63%. Mobility is thus clear, but so is the limited distance over which people travelled: almost 99% of Hutton people were Lancashire-born.

19. *The Grammar School Since 1800*

The Grammar School moved from Longton to Hutton in 1746, but during the ensuing half-century it was badly-managed and in the early 1820s the Charity Commissioners found extensive evidence of doubtful practices. School land had been let at uncommercial rates to individuals including some of the trustees themselves, or let in perpetuity, which removed the land from the control of the trustees. The trustees paid the salary of the schoolmaster at the village school in Farington (a foundation with no legal connection with the grammar school), had borrowed £500 to pay for a road through development land in Preston, and had lent large sums of money to Thomas Whitehead, the schoolmaster at Hutton, without security. The Charity Commissioners imposed a new management scheme for the school and for the other village and charity schools in Penwortham parish. Their thinking was that the local schools should be upgraded, and money from the charity specifically allocated to pay their schoolmasters, while the Grammar School would become 'a central school where the classics might be taught with its master retaining an overall superintendence of the others schools, the scholars being taught elementary and classical learning in accordance with the intent of Christopher Walton'. Schooling was to be free for scholars from Penwortham parish, and the trustees were to employ a grammar schoolmaster with a salary of £250 per annum and the use of the school house, gardens and grounds, and an under-master to be paid £90 per annum. The new scheme was implemented in August 1823 and by 1825, when the Commissioners reviewed the charity, some progress had been made, but there was still no audit of the accounts and, the Commissioners noted with particular disapproval, an annual dinner was held in a public house in Preston for the trustees, their solicitor and some of their tenants, at a cost in 1824 of £23 13s. 6d.

In August 1825 the school at Hutton had 140 pupils, both boys and girls, almost all of them being instructed in reading, writing and arithmetic on the system adopted a few years before by the National Society for the Education of the Poor in the Principles of the Established Church (founded 1811). Five boys, who boarded with Mrs Whitehead, the widow of the former master and mother of the present one, were also learning the rudiments of Latin and classical grammar. The school building had two rooms, in the upper of which the older children were taught by the master and in the lower the younger children by the usher or assistant master.[92] Despite the new management scheme, the school continued to present problems and subsequent enquiries by the Charity Commission revealed further doubtful procedures. In contrast, the reorganisation of the elementary system was more successful: in 1826 the trustees formally took over management of the school at Howick and began to pay the salary of the master, in 1829 they opened Cop Lane school to serve Penwortham township, and in 1839 began to support the Penwortham Sunday School in Priory Lane.

The real difficulty lay in the requirement that the Hutton school should teach to grammar school level. When the Schools Inquiry Commissioners made a detailed investigation in 1865 they concluded that the school was 'in a degraded condition, the work done in it being of an elementary nature, little higher in grade than that of the elementary schools at Penwortham, Farington, Howick ... and Longton'. The only efficient element in the school was a girls' elementary school, staffed by two mistresses, which had been established in the upper room of the

32. The new buildings of Hutton Grammar School, completed in 1931.

33. The chemistry laboratory at the Grammar School, 1934.

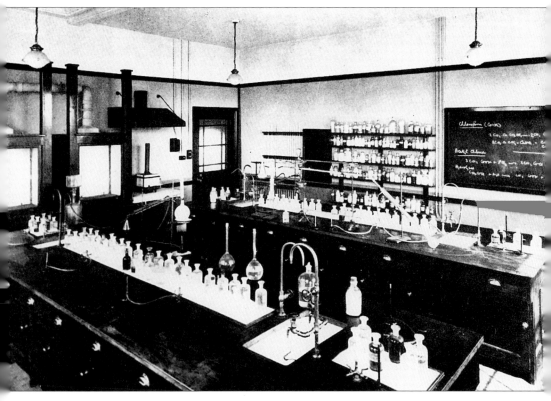

34. The Grammar School Library, 1934.

35. The dormitory for boarders at the Grammar School, 1934. (Illustrations from the 1935 school prospectus)

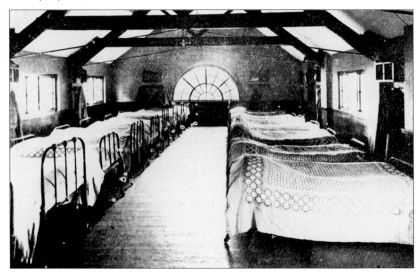

building and was technically illegal, not having been authorised under the 1825 scheme. This state of affairs was especially unacceptable because the grammar school staff were very highly paid. The headmaster had £200 a year and the usher £80 – these salaries were somewhat lower than those authorised in 1825, but the number of children had fallen by

50% since then, so they were notably generous. There had been a third master at £60 a year, but he had been pensioned off in 1860 after 56 years' continuous service – he was still teaching at the age of eighty – on an annuity of £30. All this seemed to the inspectors to be most unsatisfactory, and in 1869 the trustees, well aware of official disapproval, gave notice to the headmaster and second master because 'the condition of the school … appeared so unsatisfactory'. The headmaster, the Rev. John Ketton, had been in post since 1851 and with his large salary and comfortable rent-free house was not anxious to leave. He refused to go and ignored the dismissal order, and the affair dragged on until 1874 when, with the concurrence of the Charity Commission, he was paid £533, or two-thirds of his 1870–73 salary, in return for vacating the premises and leaving the school.

A new head was appointed and in 1876 the Charity Commissioners approved a new management scheme which regularised the legal status of the school and its managers, and established a governing body of fifteen, of whom five were ex-officio (the incumbents of Penwortham, Longton and Farington, and the lords of the manor of Penwortham and Hutton), five elected by the ratepayers of the five townships, and five co-opted. Regulations were laid down concerning the appointment of staff, including the qualifications of the headmaster, and the use of the school income. Crucially, the school was made quite distinct in character and purpose from the elementary schools within the parish, and was defined as a fee-paying grammar school. The founder's intention to provide free education to local children was deemed to have been satisfied by the provision of places in the parish schools which now came under the auspices of the charity. The school could now take boys only, from the ages of 7 to 16, at a fee of between £3 and £8 per annum, and with half-rates for children from Penwortham parish who had passed the entrance examination. It could also take boarders at a cost of £35 a year if they lodged with the headmaster and at actual cost if they lived in a hostel. The pupils would be taught in accordance with the doctrine of the Church of England, with a syllabus of reading, writing, and arithmetic; geography and history; English grammar, composition and literature; mathematics; Latin; a European language; natural science; drawing, singing and drill.

This time the new regime was effective in tackling the backlog of problems. A new Howick village school was built on the present site in

HUTTON GRAMMAR SCHOOL
School Fees, 1935

(i)	Tuition including Writing and Drawing Materials;	
	also Gymnasium and Laboratory Fees	£3 6s. 8d. per term
	If resident in County Boroughs or outside the County	
	area	£4 0s. 0d. "
(ii)	Subscription to Games and Library Fund	£0 5s. 6d. "
(iii)	Swimming: Boarders 7s. 6d: Days Bosys 6s.	
(iv)	Boarding Fees, exclusive of Tuition Fees:	
	(a) Boys under 9 years of age	£13 13s. 0d. "
	(b) Boys under 11years of age	£14 14s. 0d. "
	(c) Boys under 13 years of age	£15 15s. 0d. "
	(d) Boys over 13 years of age	£16 16s. 0d. "
	(e) Laundry and Mending	£1 7s. 6d. "
	(f) Pocket Money according to age	
	(g) Sundry Offertories	£0 2s. 0d. "
(v)	Day Boarding Fee (Dinners)	£0 1s. 0d. per day
(vi)	Charges for Optional Subjects:	
	(a) Instrumental Music (any instrument)	£2 2s. 0d. per term
	(b) Orchestral Class (String or Wood Wind)	£0 5s. 0d. "
	(c) Scouts or Cubs	£0 2s. 0d. "
	(d) Boxing	£0 18s. 0d. "

Medical Attendance and Nursing – For ordinary cases of sickness no charge is made for nursing. In cases where the services of a Doctor or Trained Nurse are required, the Fees for such are charged to Parents.

RULES FOR PAYMENT
(i) All above Fees, Subscriptions etc., are payable in advance. Termly Accounts are rendered by the Headmaster (in the case of Boarders), and the Clerk to the Governors (in the case of Day Boys), two weeks from the commencement of Term.
(ii) Journey money must be sent from home during the last week of Term and before the Half Term Holiday.
(iii) A full Term's notice in writing must be sent to the Headmaster, previous to the withdrawal of a Pupil, or failing this notice, payment of a full Term's Tuition Fees and of half a Term's Boarding Fee must be paid.

BOOKS
Text books supplied are charged in the Account. When done with, if in good condition and of use to the School, they will be bought back.

(Adapted from information in the 1935 school prospectus)

1879–1880, to serve the two townships of Howick and Hutton; the Cop Lane (Penwortham) school was rebuilt in 1881–82; new schools provided at Farington in 1882–83 and at Longton in 1892; and extensive building work undertaken at the grammar school, which was provided with a new dining room and kitchens, two dormitories to accommodate 25 boys, and in 1892 a new classroom block. To pay for all these projects, the governors sold much of the endowment land in Preston for building in the decade after 1881. By the late nineteenth century Hutton was recognisably a modern grammar school and as the curriculum expanded the range of facilities provided was increased accordingly – for example, science laboratories, a gymnasium and sports fields were added in the 1890s and early 1900s. In 1908, when the Charity Commissioners issued a consolidated report detailing all their investigations between 1850 and 1900, they concluded that the school was in excellent shape, with 78 boys of whom 48 were boarders (from as far afield as Manchester and Carlisle), and that 'the governors have for years been maintaining a first-grade school on second-grade fees ... and the scope of the school is much more ambitious than the Scheme [of 1876] contemplated'.[93]

Under the Education Act of 1902 the County Council took over the running of public secondary education, but Hutton Grammar School remained as a church foundation. During the first half of the twentieth century it continued to expand and a range of new facilities was provided between the wars, including a new complex of main school buildings in 1930–1931. Other secondary schools opened in the district, including the Penwortham Girls Grammar School, but the County Council's scheme for comprehensive education, first published in April 1976, suggested the creation of three mixed high schools for the 11–16 age group, from the Walton-le-Dale, Lostock Hall and Penwortham secondary schools, and the retention of the two grammar schools for the 11–18 age group (thus keeping sixth-forms). It was suggested that they too should become mixed schools in the future but in the initial phase retain their single-sex status.[94] This scheme came into effect in September 1978, at which point the school ceased to be selective on the grounds of ability but retained the emphasis on religious criteria in its admissions policy. Subsequently, girls were admitted to the sixth-form but the adoption of a co-educational intake from the age of 11 has not yet been implemented. At the beginning of the twenty-first century Hutton Grammar School has an enviable reputation for the quality of its teaching and educational provision: Christopher Walton would be very pleased!

20. *The Liverpool and Preston Turnpike*

The significance of the old road from Preston into south-west Lancashire grew during the eighteenth century, especially after 1753 when the Ribble was bridged at Penwortham. Its rising importance can be attributed at least in part to the development of handloom-weaving trade in the area, and to the general growth in population and commercial expansion of the county as a whole. Road improvements were already in progress in other parts of Lancashire by the 1740s, with key routes being turnpiked so that management of the road – hitherto the responsibility of individual townships – was taken over by profit-making trusts constituted by Act of Parliament and empowered to levy tolls on road-users to raise money for improvements.[95] In 1771 an Act was passed creating the Liverpool & Preston Trust, which took over the thirty miles of road between the two towns via Ormskirk and Longton. Turnpike trusts were not required by law to aim for any particular standard of improvement – what they did and when they did it was entirely up to the trustees – and so very variable standards were to be found. In Lancashire, particularly after 1790, many trusts undertook ambitious new building or greatly improved the detailed alignment of existing roads, bypassing sharp bends, widening the roads and replacing fords with bridges. There is little evidence that the Liverpool & Preston was greatly concerned to do either of these, and long stretches of its route remained as country lanes: there was better surfacing and milestones were provided but no large-scale upgrading of the road as a whole. In the mid-1820s there were proposals to build a completely new road in an almost straight line from Penwortham (Old) Bridge to the Douglas bridge at Bank Hall, but (very unfortunately in retrospect) the scheme never came to fruition. However, even the modest improvements to the old route meant that by the 1830s and 1840s the beginnings of suburban development were evident in Penwortham. In Hutton's case the advent of commuting was delayed, until the end of the nineteenth century, but it was the upgrading of the Liverpool road which made it feasible. Psychologically, perhaps, the turnpiking of the road reduced the separateness of communities such as Hutton, as well as reorientating them away from the shore-to-moss axis. For example,

37. Part of William Yates' map of Lancashire, published in 1786, showing the Hutton area with the main Preston and Liverpool turnpike road (1770) on its indirect course from the old Penwortham bridge south-west to Tarleton and the Douglas bridge. Although in the mid-1820s there were plans to build a new road in a straight line across the moss between the two bridges, the old route through the villages survived unaltered until the building of the bypasses and improvements in the 1930s and 1950s. Note also the ford which is marked crossing the Ribble sands from Hesketh Bank to Freckleton.

in 1774 the first regular stage-coach service between Liverpool and Preston began running through Hutton, and by 1800 there were four such services daily. Although the turnpike trust was dissolved in 1873, as the revenue declined with railway competition to the point where it was no longer viable, by that time Liverpool Road had become a major inter-urban trunk route, and when in the years after 1889 the County Council in stages took over the upkeep of the more important routes in its area, this was one of the first to be adopted and improved.

21. *The Ribble Navigation and its Effect on Hutton*

Throughout this history the influence of the Ribble upon Hutton has been an important theme. Today Hutton has perhaps turned its back on the river and its lifeline is a different stream – the traffic on the A59 which moves, like a tide, towards Preston in the morning and out again in the evening. This change in the orientation of Hutton was occasioned by a combination of circumstances in the later nineteenth century. Agriculture became less important to the township, as the Rawstorne estate went into the slow decline which culminated in its break-up and sale after 1915. The character of agriculture also altered. Dairying, and specifically the production of fresh milk, became more dominant in the rural economy of south Lancashire, because improved transport and refrigeration allowed the easy delivery of milk to the cities, while production of butter and cheese declined rapidly in the 1880s and 1890s in the face of competition from cheap colonial imports. Urban demand and the increased prosperity of the Lancashire working class, and the same transport and marketing improvements, encouraged the development of the market-gardening enterprises, so that by 1900 the mosslands around the Douglas and south of the Ribble were extensively used for cabbages and sprouts, leeks, carrots and celery. Elsewhere in the area, poultry-keeping became more important and this trade grew rapidly in the years before the First World War. After the war keeping chickens was seen as an essential element in a 'back to the land' movement of smallholders and small farmers.

All these changes meant that by the Edwardian period farming was in a state of transition. Land was being sold for building and development, the number of farms which needed marsh-grazing was diminishing, and although the surviving marshes are still used for this purpose (and some of them, such as Freckleton, are still regulated by committees of marsh-owners) the complex communal marsh management systems began to wane. In the case of the Ribble, though, another element entered the equation. The process of reclamation, already discussed in the context of the eighteenth-century Rawstorne documents, was accelerated by a succession of schemes for improving the river for navigation. These had the long-term effect of transforming the Hutton shore and adding hundreds of acres of new land to the parish. The first formal navigation scheme for the river was approved by parliament in 1806, proposing improvement works to regulate the difficult channel from Preston to the sea. The second largest shareholder, with six of the forty shares of £50 each, was Lawrence Rawstorne of Hutton, who here, as in other aspects of estate management, saw an opportunity for enhancing his estates as well as direct profit. Progress on the scheme was slow, but in 1807–1809 the Ribble Navigation Company cut a new channel through the Lea sands and constructed some calls (groynes) to encourage the river to adopt a straighter and more direct course.[95] A main aim of the promoters was to reclaim land on either side of the river, as had already been achieved by similar projects for navigation works on the Mersey. The principle was that, if the channel was confined so that the tide no longer spread across the marshes and mudflats, those areas could be cheaply embanked and reclaimed. The Company ran out of money in 1811, so further engineering works were impossible. The owners were hard-pressed even to maintain the buoys, beacons and other navigation aids, and cynics claimed that the whole scheme had simply been an expedient to get reclamation under way. In the late 1820s and early 1830s the Company commissioned various reports and attempted new engineering schemes, such as upgrading the quay in Preston, but the river continued to deteriorate.[96]

In 1834 proposals for a north bank ship canal from Lytham to Preston, bypassing the river altogether, were seriously considered. Although this did not come to fruition, Preston Corporation sponsored a report in 1837 which proposed a combination of a new and deep-dredged channel from Preston quay, where a new enclosed dock was to be constructed, down to Freckleton Naze. The channel would be excavated by steam-dredging machines and maintained by dredging, and the cost of construction was put – optimistically in the extreme – at only £30,000. This report specifically rejected the idea of reclaiming the shallows on either side of the new channel. A new Navigation Company was formed

and in 1838 the proposals received parliamentary approval. The old
company was bought out and in its successor the largest single shareholder
by far was Preston Corporation (with 21% of the shareholding). Among
the gentlemen who subscribed, and who sat on the first board of directors,
was Lawrence Rawstorne. The second Ribble Navigation Company cut
a new channel in stages from Ashton Marsh towards the Naze, combining
this with a programme of dredging. Major investment at the Preston

38. Part of Greenwood's map of Lancashire, published in 1818, showing the unimproved
Ribble estuary with its winding channel and sandbanks. This landscape was about to
disappear, for in the next half-century schemes to make the river navigable for larger vessels
would result in the straightening of the channel, and after 1885 a completely new embanked
course would be constructed with the large area of marshland on either side reclaimed and
converted into fields. Also shown on this map is the small area of surviving mossland south
of Chain House and Whitestake, the last vestige of the great mosses of South Ribble. It, too,
disappeared in the next thirty years.

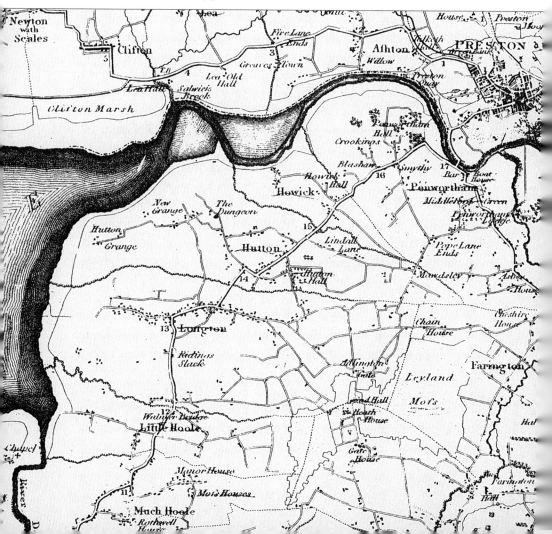

end created a new Victoria Quay, warehouses, and other facilities, so that by 1846 the town was experiencing encouraging growth as a port. Crucially, by 1850 embankments had been constructed on both sides of the river from Ashton down to Freckleton and Hutton, constraining the dredged channel and preventing even the higher tides from flowing over substantial areas of saltmarsh on both sides of the river. Reclamation of these areas to create improved pasture now seemed feasible, even though it was not part of the original plan. The new embankments withstood a series of floods and very high tides in late 1840s and an engineer's report of 1850 discussed in detail the progress of the reclamation, noting that the natural deposition of sand and silt in the area enclosed by the new embankments was proceeding apace.

It was calculated that, only five years after the works were started, 1188 acres of the estuary were now dry enough to support vegetation, and another 4000 acres were likely to be reclaimable in due course. At Hutton, the report stated, new marsh was developing near the Howick boundary and closer inshore, and 'since the completion of the cross-embankment betwixt Hutton and Howick, the rise of the sands in the upper part of Hutton, has been very quick and will shortly be up to the level of the river walls; the margin of vegetation upon this marsh is extending itself, year by year'. In total, 139 acres were being reclaimed in Hutton, and a further 760 acres would eventually be feasible. Because of the problem of finance and the need to establish a clear legal title to the reclaimed lands, a new Act of Parliament was passed in February 1854, by which the second Navigation Company was dissolved and a third created. The new Company's Act of Parliament had stated that the reclaimed land was to be vested in the ownership of the Company itself, but that the adjacent landowners had the right to purchase it. In the case of Howick the land remained in Company ownership and was a useful source of additional finance for the Company, but Lawrence Rawstorne exercised his right to acquire the newly-reclaimed marsh at Hutton and in 1855 he bought 90 acres for £1,184.

During the 1860s further dredging and embankment-building added to the reclaimed area on the Hutton and Longton boundary, extending dry land out into the centre of the old estuary. The final stage in the development of the Navigation was the construction of Preston Dock and the further reinforcement of the embankments and walls from the dock to Freckleton Naze and Hutton, in 1885–1892. There were large-scale works in the outer estuary – the building of training walls and alteration of the channels – and as a consequence of all these works the area of the drained and enclosed land in Hutton has been greatly increased, although there are still extensive areas of marsh beyond the embankments. These tracts of semi-dry land, extending almost as far as the confluence of the two rivers, lie across what was until a hundred years ago the Hutton Sands in the open estuary, and they result from natural accretion processes in the aftermath of the navigation works. This area of marsh is therefore directly the consequence of man's activities and, as many observers have recently noted, their future is uncertain. The end of dredging and the abandonment of the channel as a commercial waterway have resulted in changes to the outer estuary as the river reasserts itself, seeking to return to its natural channel. As the outer training walls erode and disappear, tidal action against the embankments and marshes of the middle estuary may increase and, if sea levels rise rapidly during the next half century, the sustainability of such man-made land is open to question.

22. The West Lancashire Railway

The area between Preston and Southport was not an obvious target for railway promoters in the mid-nineteenth century, since it lacked major centres of population and had no industrial potential. From time to time proposals were put forward for a route between the two towns along the south shore of the river, but not until August 1871 was the West Lancashire Railway incorporated for this purpose. The territory was unpromising, and the line characterises the second great phase of railway development, which involving filling the gaps on the map. Most obvious routes linking major traffic generators had long since been built, and speculative promotion now focussed on competitive routes or on schemes with limited commercial viability. The potential traffic was modest – agricultural produce, especially milk, eggs, vegetables and fruit; bricks from the Longton area and possibly transshipped goods from the little river port at Tarleton on the Douglas, and perhaps some inter-urban passenger traffic between Preston and Southport. Rural agricultural lines

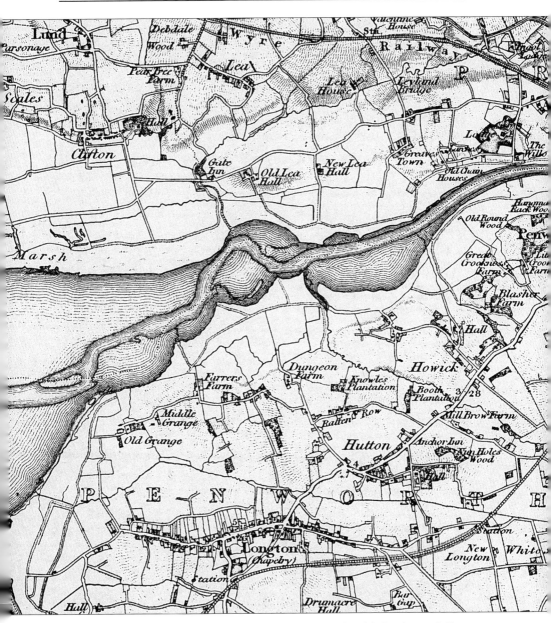

39. The Ordnance Survey map (1-inch to 1-mile) of 1845 was updated during the next half century by the inclusion of new railway lines even though the basic mapping was unaltered. In this extract the landscape is essentially that of the mid-1840s, but the West Lancashire Railway of 1882 has been added. It followed a lazy course across the flat countryside on the south side of the river, linking Preston and Southport. The stations at Longton and Hutton (then called Howick) are marked on the map, though it is clear that the latter station (actually in the parish of Longton) was 'in the middle of nowhere'.

were numerous in the later nineteenth century and, almost without exception, were commercial failures. In the case of the West Lancashire, failure was apparent even before opening, for it took seven years to raise the capital and construct the first seven miles, from Hesketh Park in Southport to Hesketh Bank. Given the fact that almost no major engineering works were needed, this was small progress indeed. Work then ceased while more money was raised, and another four years elapsed before the remainder of the line was completed: in May 1882 the bridge across the Douglas and the line as far as Longton were opened, and in September of the same year the sections from Longton to Fishergate Hill in Preston and into Southport Central were completed. It had taken eleven years to build thirteen miles of line. The West Lancashire Railway originally had a stations at Hoole and Longton, but in 1889 another was opened at Chapel Lane crossing in the parish of Longton. It was called – rather oddly – Howick, but ten years later was renamed Hutton & Howick and in 1924 became New Longton.

The effect of the railway on the neighbourhood was predictably limited. Traffic levels were disastrously low, and the company has been described as 'a poverty-stricken concern which never paid a dividend and was unable to keep up its debenture payments'. After promoting a few wild schemes for extensions to Blackpool and Wigan, the company was bought out by the Lancashire & Yorkshire in July 1897 and the line settled down to a peaceful and unassuming existence as a rural backwater. The existence of the station at Hutton & Howick, like that at Longton, generated a modest suburban traffic and it is this that was primarily responsible for the initial growth of New Longton, which began to develop as a separate community in the years before the First World War. The promotional literature and sales catalogues for estate and land sales in Hutton between 1915 and 1935 regularly emphasise the convenience of having the station nearby, and this was also mentioned as a reason for the choice of Hutton as the site of the county's agricultural college. The line closed in September 1964 and over long stretches its route has almost disappeared, but the Cop Lane section of the Penwortham 'bypass' and the underpass on the Longton bypass at Chapel Lane are the most obvious legacy of its existence today. Ironically, had it survived a few years longer, the increasing traffic congestion in Preston and Southport and the 1980s revival in rail passenger traffic would perhaps have given it a role which it never enjoyed in its 82 years of working life.[97]

23. *Hutton Parish Council, 1895–1922*

On 1 January 1895, under the terms of the Local Government Act of 1894, Hutton, like thousands of other rural communities across the country, became a civil parish with a democratically-elected parish council. The new council, which first met on 17 February 1895, had six members and, in keeping with the squirarchical world of the late Victorian countryside, Lawrence Rawstorne was chosen as the first chairman, a position which he held continuously until 1914. Each year the council chose a treasurer, an overseer and a waywarden (to look after the highways) and, because of the very small number of councillors, these offices circulated each year among the same handful of men, most of them the leading farmers of the parish. The 1894 Act also established rural districts with elected councils, and Hutton was included with its neighbours as part of the new Preston Rural District, an awkward administrative unit which fell into two unconnected parts, south of the Ribble and in the Chipping and Goosnargh area. The parish council would have preferred a more local unit and in April 1899, when it was it proposed that the Preston RDC should take over the management and maintenance of the roads from the parish councils, petitioned with Longton and Penwortham for the creation of a separate rural district for the seven parishes between the Ribble and the Douglas. This was denied and the rural district council assumed responsibility for highways, thus removing one of the few serious functions which parish councils had exercised. The idea of a separate district council for the ancient parish of Penwortham did not disappear – Hutton Parish Council was pressing for this again in 1924–1930.[98]

Perhaps because the parish council had few real powers, and there was little business in this small community, there was no enthusiasm for its activities. Apart from the occasional discussion of the state of a public footpath, or the blocking of a ditch, business was confined to the formal appointment of a chairman and overseer and the setting of a tiny rate. As late as 1921 the annual administrative costs of the parish council were a mere £1 10s. 3d. (£1.51), of which 10s. was the clerk's honorarium and another 10s. the cost of the obligatory audit of the

HUTTON
Private residents and farmers in 1885

NB. Directories only included residents of some social standing, together with traders and farmers. Ordinary villagers are not listed.

Ball, William (blacksmith)
Cank, Thomas (gamekeeper)
Clegg, George (victualler, *Blue Anchor*)
Hutton Grammar School:
   Rev. B. C. Huntly, headmaster;
   W. H. Culverwell, second master;
   French master, Mons. F.E. Bazin;
   Junior master, John Hall;
   drawing master, Wm. Bowness-
    Burton;
   music master, W. Ffoulkes;
   drill instructor, Sergeant Gregory;

medical officer, R. C. Brown Esq.,
   M.B. (Lond.).
Murray, John, steward to L. Rawstorne
   Esq.
Norris, William, timekeeper
Singleton, Mrs Margaret
Smalley, Mr Thomas, Rose cottage
Smith, Mrs Ann, shopkeeper
Taylor, John, basket maker
Threllfall, Mr Wm, Holly house

Farmers

Ball, John (Carr's farm)
Beesley, James (Woodfold farm)
Blackhurst, David
Blundell, Thomas (Cook's farm)
Calderbank, Richard (School house farm)
Clark, Watson (Tithebarn)
Clegg, James
Clegg, John and Margaret (Lane end)
Cook, Thomas (Lane end)
Coxhead, Mrs Isabella (Lindle lane)
Fazackerley, Jane, Brick hill
Fisher, Thomas (Sheardley's farm)
Heaton, Richard (Moor farm)
Hesketh, Henry (Dungeon farm)
Hodge, Henry (New House farm)
Howcroft, John (Mill Brow farm)
Houghton, John (Hesketh's farm)
Knowles, Robert (Nook farm)
Moss, Thomas (Skip lane)
Rawcliffe, Ann (Lindle lane)

Rawcliffe, Mrs Ellen (Nutter's platt)
Rawcliffe, John (Hesketh's)
Sanderson, Andrew (Cockerton's farm)
Scarlett, John (Bambford's farm)
Sergeant, Richard (Middle grange)
Singleton, Thomas (Lindle lane)
Slater, Alice
Slater, John
Slater, Robert
Slater, William
Smalley, John & George (White coppice)
Smith, Edward (Knowles farm)
Stephenson, Alexander [hind] (Old
   Grange)
Tattersall, Mrs Ann (Thistle farm)
Walmsley, James
Whittle, Mrs Ellen (Workhouse farm)
Wilson, Hugh (Workhouse farm)
Wilding, Thomas (Smithy farm)
Worthington, Robert

Adapted from Barrett's *History and Directory of Preston and The Fylde (1885)*

accounts. Before the First World War the council often met only once a year, and in 1905 and 1906 does not seem to have met at all – certainly no minutes were entered for those two years. Councillors were elected at the annual parish meeting, and in March 1913 the election was declared null and void because the overseer (who acted as returning officer) failed to bring sufficient nomination papers. The re-run in early April was also declared void, since too few ratepayers were present for the meeting to be quorate, and it was not until the end of April that a proper and legitimate election was achieved. There is no evidence that anybody was unduly concerned!

At the parish meeting in March 1919 only eight people were present. The chairman, the Rev. Thomas Cunningham, handed in the nomination papers and fifteen minutes elapsed, during which time other nominations could be received from the floor. No name was put forward, so the chairman read out the names of the five candidates for the five places, declaring them to be elected. Any ratepayer had the constitutional right to demand that a ballot be held, so another pause of ten minutes was allowed: no poll was demanded, the election was completed, and the meeting then closed. At this meeting, however, there was one particular difference. Among the councillors elected was a woman, and a remarkable woman at that. Mrs Edith Rigby, of Marigold Cottage in Howick, was a local celebrity, a campaigner for women's rights and before the war a suffragette. Her arrival among the solid farmers of Hutton caused something of a stir, and there is some evidence that after the 1919 election the Council was more active – certainly, Mrs Rigby's questions about housing shortages, the untidy state of the roadsides and the problems of sanitation made a change from no business at all. She only stayed on the Parish Council for three years, but by that time the winds of change were blowing ever stronger in Hutton, and things would never be the same again.[99]

24. *The Start of Change: Land Sales and Building Schemes, 1895–1920*

While the parish council was largely inactive before the 1920s, the district council was concerned with the provision of modern public services, albeit with a conspicuous reluctance to spend ratepayers' money. The annual reports of the Medical Officer of Health give valuable information about its activities, and sometimes comment sharply on the way in which

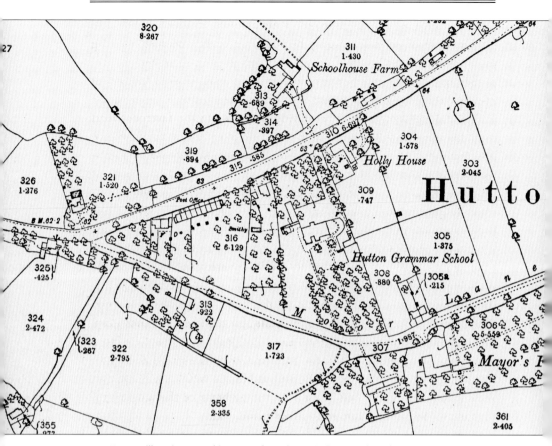

41. Hutton village in 1895: this extract from the 25-inch to 1-mile Ordnance Survey map shows how a hundred years ago the township was still a rural community, although within fifty years it would have been totally transformed by housing development. The Grammar School is prominent in the centre and the long narrow plots of land on the north side of Liverpool Road mark the enclosures of the former broad roadside verges which took place in the seventeenth century. At the south-east corner of the extract is Mayor's Farm (now Hutton Manor) which – contrary to its name – was never the manor house, although it is now probably the best-preserved of all the older farmhouses in the parish.

changes were taking place in the rural areas around Preston. Public health in the countryside had long been a matter of concern, but the spectacularly bad situation in the towns and cities (Preston was notoriously unhealthy) tended to monopolise popular attention. The first Medical Officer of Health for Preston RDC, Charles Trimble, served for the extraordinary period of 59 years, during most of which time he was also MOH for Walton-le-Dale and Fulwood Urban District Councils. He endeavoured to persuade the authorities to implement basic schemes, such as sewage disposal, which would improve health and provide modern facilities. Usually he was unsuccessful, because reducing the rates was a priority for both central and local government.

During the mid-1890s Preston Corporation's Waterworks Department was extending its area of supply, building a new large pipe across the Ribble at Penwortham and then laying mains along the Liverpool road to Longton. This scheme served Hutton en route and at first, because householders had to pay for connections, the take-up was slow. Hutton was comparatively healthy, with a low death rate and low incidence of notifiable disease,[100] so individual residents felt little need to switch from well water to mains supplies. By the end of 1901 only 48 houses had been connected and, since similar reluctance was apparent in neighbouring places, the MOH was scathing in his comments: 'the tenacity is positively ridiculous, if not almost criminal, with which some people will cling to old-fashioned and dangerous sources of water ... [I] am constantly met with the defence that the water in question has been used for generations without any dire results'. He deplored 'such obstinacy and love of accepting risks in the most blind fashion to avoid paying a moderate water rate'.[101] The extension of the mains continued after 1900: by 1905, 76 of the 86 inhabited houses in Hutton had been connected, and by 1910, 100 of the 108 houses. At the outbreak of the war in 1914 all but two houses in Hutton were on mains water.

With its small population and entirely rural character the public health of Hutton did not at this stage give rise to concern, in marked contrast to the position in Penwortham and Longton where urban development and rapid growth were not matched by the provision of modern sewerage and water supply systems. In 1903 the MOH noted the dangers to public health in those two parishes, and before the First World War he highlighted the need for proper services throughout the area between the Ribble and Longton. At the end of the Edwardian era the development of Hutton as a residential area became a probability – between 1905 and 1914 the number of inhabited houses in the parish rose from 86 to 117, a modest increase but one which emphasises that change was under way for growth increase on this scale was unprecedented. In 1910 (in what was possibly the first-ever use of the name 'South Ribble') the MOH pointed to the development potential of Hutton itself: 'the South Ribble area is selected for the erection of dwelling houses ... the villas now being constructed about Hutton and Howick, and in Chapel Lane, are

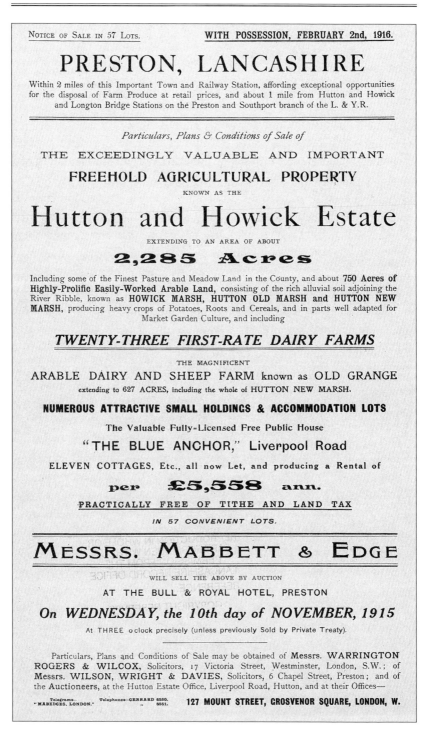

NOTICE OF SALE IN 57 LOTS.   WITH POSSESSION, FEBRUARY 2nd, 1916.

PRESTON, LANCASHIRE

Within 2 miles of this Important Town and Railway Station, affording exceptional opportunities for the disposal of Farm Produce at retail prices, and about 1 mile from Hutton and Howick and Longton Bridge Stations on the Preston and Southport branch of the L. & Y.R.

Particulars, Plans & Conditions of Sale of

THE EXCEEDINGLY VALUABLE AND IMPORTANT

FREEHOLD AGRICULTURAL PROPERTY

KNOWN AS THE

Hutton and Howick Estate

EXTENDING TO AN AREA OF ABOUT

2,285 Acres

Including some of the Finest Pasture and Meadow Land in the County, and about **750 Acres of Highly-Prolific Easily-Worked Arable Land,** consisting of the rich alluvial soil adjoining the River Ribble, known as **HOWICK MARSH, HUTTON OLD MARSH and HUTTON NEW MARSH,** producing heavy crops of Potatoes, Roots and Cereals, and in parts well adapted for Market Garden Culture, and including

TWENTY-THREE FIRST-RATE DAIRY FARMS

THE MAGNIFICENT

ARABLE DAIRY AND SHEEP FARM known as OLD GRANGE

extending to 627 ACRES, including the whole of HUTTON NEW MARSH.

NUMEROUS ATTRACTIVE SMALL HOLDINGS & ACCOMMODATION LOTS

The Valuable Fully-Licensed Free Public House

"THE BLUE ANCHOR," Liverpool Road

ELEVEN COTTAGES, Etc., all now Let, and producing a Rental of

per £5,558 ann.

PRACTICALLY FREE OF TITHE AND LAND TAX

IN 57 CONVENIENT LOTS.

MESSRS. MABBETT & EDGE

WILL SELL THE ABOVE BY AUCTION

AT THE BULL & ROYAL HOTEL, PRESTON

On WEDNESDAY, the 10th day of NOVEMBER, 1915

At THREE o'clock precisely (unless previously Sold by Private Treaty).

Particulars, Plans and Conditions of Sale may be obtained of Messrs. **WARRINGTON ROGERS & WILCOX,** Solicitors, 17 Victoria Street, Westminster, London, S.W.; of Messrs. **WILSON, WRIGHT & DAVIES,** Solicitors, 6 Chapel Street, Preston; and of the Auctioneers, at the Hutton Estate Office, Liverpool Road, Hutton, and at their Offices—

Telegrams—   Telephones—GERRARD 8550.
" MABEDGES, LONDON."   " 8551.   **127 MOUNT STREET, GROSVENOR SQUARE, LONDON, W.**

nice, well-put-together houses, and must be both healthy and comfortable'. Three years later he correctly identified that the new bridge between Penwortham and Preston (finally opened in 1915) would transform the area by making it accessible to commuters and noted that this process was already under way: 'the people living there are what may be termed "Residentials", as the bread winners to a large extent have their businesses and work in Preston [I cite] Penwortham and Hutton and Howick'. With these developments in mind, the Preston RDC began preliminary design work for a new sewerage scheme which would serve Penwortham, Hutton and Longton.[102]

All these actual or potential developments gave the necessary context for housing development, but there was an even more essential ingredient – the availability of land. As long as the Rawstorne estate remained intact, and was farmed as a large landholding, the scale of building would remain modest. However, in 1915 the Rawstorne family put the property on the market and opened the door for large-scale residential development and speculative building. Hutton could have experienced the transformation which Penwortham and Longton had encountered in the years after 1880. The disposal of the agricultural estate at Hutton was managed by Mabbett and Edge, agents and auctioneers of Grosvenor Square in London, and their sales catalogue draws attention to the potential for residential development as well as describing the more conventional attributes and advantages of the land for farming. The estate was divided up into 57 lots, ranging from individual cottages to the 627 acres of Old Grange Farm, and some of those which lay along or close to Liverpool road were singled out as prime building land. Thus, Anchor Field, in the angle of Liverpool Road and Ratten Row, offered 'an exceptional opportunity for profitable and economical development for building purposes', while Tithebarn Farm, with its frontage of 1300 feet on the Liverpool road, included 'splendid old meadows and rich pasture land' much of which was 'Ripe for Building Purposes'.[103] The tone of the catalogue implied that farming would still be the main attraction, but the estate was being broken up and the experience of

42 (*opposite*). The break-up and sale of the Rawstorne estate took place in stages between 1894 and 1922. In 1915 the majority of the property north of Liverpool Road was advertised for sale and at the subsequent auction was purchased by Captain Waring, who resold it to the County Council in 1919. This illustration shows the title page of the auction catalogue. (From LRO DDX 74/16/7)

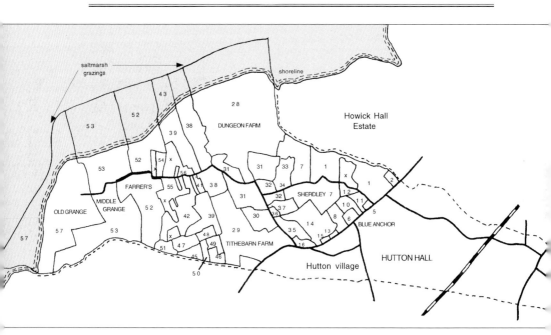

43. The lots offered for sale when the majority of the remaining Rawstorne estate was put
up for auction in 1915. From this map it is clear not only that major farms, such as those
along Grange Lane, were to be sold in their entirety, but also that along Liverpool Road small
lots were offered with an eye on the small speculative housebuilder.

comparable communities elsewhere suggested that house-building was a
strong possibility. However, the sale took place during the First World
War and purchase for immediate building was not realistic, because
wartime restrictions on building prevented any such aspiration. Much
of the estate was instead bought for speculation by Captain Waring and
was resold by him to the County Council in 1919.

25. The County Council Farm and the Agricultural College

Change had already affected the parish in other ways. On its creation
at the beginning of 1889 Lancashire County Council established a Technical Instruction Committee, charged with the task of developing schemes
for vocational training in agriculture and crafts. In the spring of 1891

44. Edward Beattie's 1899 drawing of the Home Farm, Hutton Hall, which in 1894 had been bought, together with 157 acres of excellent farmland, by Lancashire County Council to form the basis of the new agricultural college. (From LRO CC/TIR/3, Annual Report of the County Technical Instruction Committee)

the Committee approved a programme of lectures in subjects such as cheese- and butter-making and dairying,[104] holding classes in places as diverse (and in some cases as non-agricultural) as Ulverston, Oswald-twistle and Ashton-in-Makerfield. Two years later a more permanent and very successful 'cheese and butter school' was opened on William Allsupp's farm at Preece Hall near Kirkham and the county started to give grants to the Harris Institute in Preston for providing instructors and examining candidates. The programme was extended to include bee-keeping, horticulture, veterinary science and grassland improvement, and as student numbers grew the Committee decided to acquire its own farm and run the scheme directly. A joint meeting with the Harris Institute in October 1893 resolved that a farm 'for instructional, experimental and illustrative purposes should be taken, in order to make sufficient provision for Agricultural Instruction, practical as well as theoretical'.

In February 1894 a shortlist of four possible sites, at Hutton, Lea Road, Broughton and Alston Hall, was considered, and Hutton was eventually selected because it was 'situated near the town of Preston, from which it was distant by an excellent road about three and a half miles. Howick Station, on the West Lancashire Railway, was on the outskirts of the farm, and distant from the Homestead less than half a mile, whilst the Longton Station, on the same railway – where there were goods sidings – was within one and a half miles'. The property had a good farmhouse, and another house occupied by the head cowman; an excellent dairy with marble slabs and glazed with encaustic tiles; a wash-house; and a farmyard and associated buildings ranged around three sides of a square, with a passageway running their full length fitted with a tramway and turntables from which cattle stalls and horse boxes could be supplied with feed via a tilting wagon. There was space for forty cattle; four feeding boxes; three large pens for young cattle; five calf pens; a loose box for a bull; a mixing room and granary for fodder; a root house to store worzels and other feed; stables, harness room and loose boxes; a covered manure tank in the centre of the yard; a four-bay Dutch barn; an engine-shed with saw benches and other equipment; and a carpenter's shop, slaughter house and poultry house. The farm had been largely rebuilt in 1875, so everything was in good repair, and with it came 147 acres of 'superior land' excellent potential for the dairying which would be the main aim of the project. The terms were favourable – a rental of £400 per annum for a twenty year lease – and the agreement to take the farm as a going concern was signed in March 1894.[105]

Day-to-day management was overseen by a committee comprised of county councillors and representatives from the Harris Institute and the Royal Lancashire Agricultural Society. The venture was challenging and this pioneering project in public involvement in agriculture attracted widespread interest. The Harris Institute provided the lecturers and there was frequent emphasis in the reports and minutes on the need for high standards and proper examination procedures. This early attention to quality ensured that from the start the County Farm had a high reputation within the trade and also locally. By the summer of 1894 much produce – butter, cheese, eggs, cream and milk – was being sold to 'casual visitors' for whom the guaranteed quality was a major attraction, town suppliers being markedly less assiduous in their attention to hygiene and food standards. The 1895 Report to the Technical Instruction Committee recorded that farm had already sold nearly 12,000lb of cheese and butter, with another 7,500lb in stock, and that cream, milk and eggs were also regularly produced for commercial or private sale. In 1897

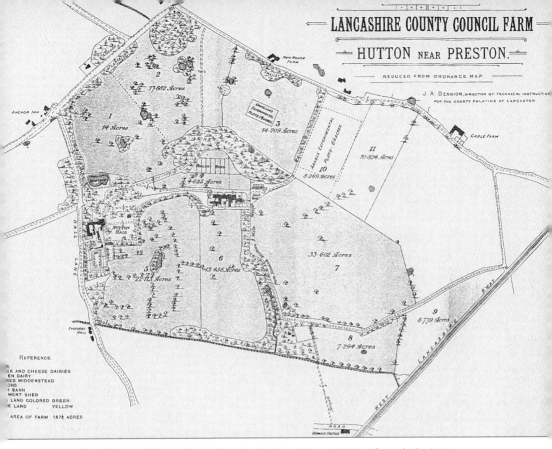

45. An 1899 map of the new Lancashire County Council Farm at Hutton, formerly the Home Farm of the Rawstorne family's Hutton Hall estate. The sale of this land to the County Council marked the first major stage in the break-up and disposal of the estate which the family had held for 350 years, since 1547. (From LRO CC/TIR/3, Annual Report of the County Technical Instruction Committee)

it was reported that 12,159lb of Lancashire cheese was sold, but also 5,600lb of Camembert, Gorgonzola, Port du Salut, Coulommier, Little Gloucester, Caerphilly and Derby – there was no protection of regional trade names in the Europe of 1897! [106]

For the County Council the running of the farm posed unexpected headaches, including one with which its members were certainly not familiar: how to regulate student behaviour. At the beginning of the twenty-first century, further education, with students living in college, is a commonplace, but when the farm was established there were few universities and residential colleges were scarcely contemplated. There was particular concern about the fact that this was a co-educational institution, and the folly of allowing male and female students to mix was frequently a matter of discussion. For example, in May 1894, when the classes were being set up, it was agreed that 'Male & Female Pupils be not received in the Dairy Schools at the same time & that no Male Classes be held at present' – perhaps the notion of a male dairymaid was too radical to contemplate – but such rules were there to be breached, and in March 1895 it was ordered that Miss Macqueen, the dairying teacher, 'be authorised to make such regulations for the restriction of the female students from holding conversation with the Workmen & Male Students on the Farm as she may deem desirable'. As far as we can tell, these efforts met with no success.[107]

26. *The County Council Smallholdings*

The success of the farm at Hutton was a major factor in the continued interest in agriculture which was maintained by the County Council. The council several times considered buying land and letting out small-holdings to labourers, but nothing tangible was achieved before the outbreak of the First World War. In 1918 the Small Holding Colonies (Amendment) Act was passed to encourage the provision of smallholdings for unemployed ex-servicemen, a scheme derived in part from a naively idealistic 'back to the land' movement. Government loans were provided for county councils to purchase land, erect buildings and divide the property into smaller units, and for loans to individuals for start-up costs. In December 1918 Lancashire allocated £50,000 for this purpose and within six months had received 573 applications from ex-servicemen. Among the sites chosen was the Hutton and Howick estate, which was placed on the market by Captain Waring who had purchased it from the Rawstornes in 1915. The county's agent negotiated a purchase price of £102,500, for which sum the Council acquired 1,914 acres of land, divided into twelve farms, together with the freehold of the Blue Anchor Inn at Hutton.[108]

The county took possession on 2 February 1920, and tackled a large backlog of neglect. According to the county land agent, the land was overrun with rabbits and hares; the embankments on the marsh were undermined by rats and moles; field drains were collapsing; the sluices and ditches were choked and impeding drainage off the land; and the ploughing of 1919 had not been followed by seeding so that weed growth was rampant. During the summer of 1920 women and schoolboys were employed to clear the land of docks and other weeds, steam-powered excavators dug new ditches and cleared the existing channels, farm roads were upgraded, and the land was deep ploughed with steam tractors. In December 1920 it was reported that the staff had made up nearly two miles of road, cleaned two miles of ditches, put up new fencing and laid new field drains, repaired all the farm buildings and sown nearly 1000 acres with crops and hay grass. By that time 423 acres had been let and most of the remainder was now in a suitable condition to be offered to potential tenants.

One advantage of this estate was that there already 12 farms and several labourers' cottages, some of which were vacant, so it was possible to bring in some new tenants reasonably soon. The longer term plan was that the land should be subdivided, with, in Hutton parish, ten cottage-holdings of cottage, garden and 0–3 acres of land; 15 smallholdings of cottage, garden and 4–10 acres of land; two smallholdings of 11–20 acres; one smallholding of 21–30 acres; and four smallholdings of 31–40 acres. There would also be two smallholdings of 41–50 acres on the Howick part of the estate. In all, this would require the building of 29 new cottage dwellings, with another five adapted from four existing cottages on the estate. There would also be four new sets of farm buildings, as well as seven sets of buildings converted from five existing farms, and a further 23 sets of new wooden farm buildings for poultry and outhouses. The County Council would also have to provide roads and services, drainage facilities, water supplies and other infrastructure, and work on the smallholdings went ahead during 1921. However, the ministry insisted that, in order to reduce costs, the original plans should be modified to exclude Grange Farm, which at 667 acres represented by far the largest individual component of the estate.[109]

New houses were built during 1921, including 13 four-bedroomed properties constructed of ferro-concrete and four wooden bungalows in Ratten Lane, converted from temporary huts. Wranglings with the ministry continued, as the county attempted to sell the Grange Farm property on the open market in order to defray the costs of the remainder of the scheme. The farm was offered for sale at auction in August 1921 but failed to reach the reserve price and another auction attempt in May 1922 also failed. It was not until October 1922 that it was eventually

46. First Preston, and then Penwortham, grew rapidly in the nineteenth century, and farms in areas such as Hutton and Longton soon developed profitable new businesses supplying fresh food and milk to the householders of the town. This picture shows Mr Jackson of Cockerton Farm in about 1900, with a horse-drawn milk float which had been originally made for Mary Clegg of the *Blue Anchor* Inn; Mr Jackson used it for milk deliveries in Penwortham.

disposed of for £19,500 to Vestey Brothers after the county had had to include in the sale another 22 acres of pasture and its leasehold interest in the 237 acres of grazing land and outmarsh on the Hutton and Howick Marshes.

The County Council was evidently finding that what had seemed a relatively simple project was proving to be a financial and administrative nightmare. The parsimony of the ministry (which had very quickly lost its initial enthusiasm for the national smallholdings scheme) was exacerbated by local difficulties as the land proved to need much more investment than was at first realised. In the autumn of 1921, for example, it was reported that the drainage works undertaken in the previous year were inadequate and that a comprehensive scheme for the entire estate was required. The ministry refused to sanction the expenditure and during 1922 a much less satisfactory piecemeal project was implemented. Progress was thus faltering and the optimism of 1918 had long since faded by the autumn of 1923, when the scheme was completed and a total of 69 smallholdings and farm units had been established and tenanted. Hutton was not the only site in Lancashire being developed as smallholding but it was by a considerable measure the largest and most complex. Ultimately the project must be judged at best only a partial success, not just because of ministry obstructiveness but also because nationally the 1920s' enthusiasm for smallholdings as a panacea for post-war economic and social problems quickly proved to be an illusion. Those who took on tenancies were often unable to cope with the hardships of farming, while the financial collapse of the late 1920s disrupted agricultural economics to an unmanageable extent. Agriculture itself was changing as mechanisation, the increasingly international nature of food trading, and the development of large-scale retailing and market- ing altered the circumstances within which smallholders operated. It was a brave and well-meant experiment, but one which in retrospect can be seen as ill-fated from the beginning.[110]

27. *The Police Headquarters*

In the late 1920s Lancashire County Council was therefore already the owner of a substantial part of Hutton and, when the possibility of building a new police headquarters was raised, the search for sites eventually focussed on the parish. The remainder of the former Rawstorne estate was coming on the market and Hutton seemed destined to be particularly well-suited for road communications under the ambitious highway strategies being proposed in the early 1930s. In 1937 the county bought Hutton Hall and the adjacent Moor Farm, to provide sites for the new police headquarters and also for the proposed Longton bypass, and in 1938 the scale of the project was substantially increased when the county also bought the Holme Mead estate to accommodate the mounted division, bringing the land acquisitions to a total of 141 acres. In August 1938 the Home Secretary approved the principle of the project and a design competition was held for a scheme which included not only the new headquarters but also a police training centre, service facilities, a motor patrol centre and a range of ancillary buildings, all in a landscaped setting.[111]

In May 1937 a group of Lancashire officers attended a driving course at Hendon and immediately afterwards established a new police driving school at Hutton Hall, which had just passed into county ownership. In July 1937 a large garage block for eighteen instruction vehicles was completed, and preliminary work on the headquarters was scheduled to start in the early summer of 1939. Because of the national emergency, the police committee and the Home Office decided to delay work on the project and instead the garage block was converted quickly and cheaply as offices and emergency planning rooms for wartime use. The vehicles were moved out in September 1939 and at the same time Hutton Hall was taken over as an interim police headquarters, with special private telephone links throughout the county. The additional conversion work was undertaken as a matter of urgency, beginning on the day that war broke out, and in March 1940 the police moved from County Hall to Hutton. After the war, despite further delays caused by the moratorium on public building and by the shortage of fuel and materials, progress was made on constructing almost fifty police houses on the estate.

The original plans were finally implemented in 1959–61, when the three hundred year old Hutton Hall was demolished and much of its fine landscaped grounds cleared to make way for the large new complex of headquarters buildings. The new driving school at Moor Farm was completed soon afterwards. Since that time, as the needs of the police service have grown and altered almost beyond recognition, a variety of additional buildings and major new communications facilities have been added to the complex, which is today perhaps the most familiar landmark in Hutton for most people passing by on the busy A59.[112]

28. Housing Development between the 1920s and 1970s

The purchase of much of the Rawstorne estate by the County Council in 1919 for the smallholdings scheme meant that a substantial part of Hutton was, for the time being at least, unavailable for development, but other parts of the estate were sold for building in 1922. In that year E. J. Reed of Fishergate in Preston offered 53 acres of 'eligible building land' in six lots, situated in the vicinity of Liverpool Road, Hutton Row and Moor Lane. The 1922 sale catalogue made little effort to market the land for anything but development purposes, and the properties were bought by various local builders for whom they were an opportunity

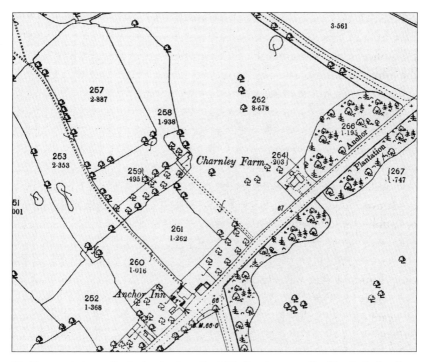

47. The area between the *Anchor Inn* (usually at this time known as the *Blue Anchor*) and Ratten Lane in 1895, from the Ordnance Survey 25-inch to 1-mile sheet. The small fields behind the inn and around Charnley Farm were sold for building development in 1915, and between the wars many new houses were built in this part of Hutton. The map also shows the woodland which had been planted along the main road frontage in the early nineteenth century as part of the landscaping of the Hutton Hall estate. Some of this woodland survives today as the fine trees along the central reservation and south side of the dual-carriageway main road, having been preserved as an amenity when the road-widening was undertaken at the end of the 1930s.

to cash in on the growing trend among the professional and managerial classes towards living well away from the workplace, in attractive semi-rural locations. The promotional literature for the sale emphasised the convenience of the site, close to Hutton & Howick railway station and well-served by motorbus routes. The mobility which was afforded to a few by the railway, to many by the motor bus, and to an increasing minority by the motor car, meant that living in Hutton and working in Preston was now feasible. The parcels sold in 1922 were comparatively small. For example, Lots 1 and 2, with a total area of seven acres, were described in the sale catalogue as 'a capital building site' enjoying a 490 foot frontage on Liverpool Road: such a location was of major importance to small builders, because main roads were already serviced and so the extra cost of providing water and other utilities was greatly reduced. On these two plots, which were sold as one block, the first major new development within the parish, Tolsey Drive, was built in 1924–1927. This was soon followed by the sale for building of the land around the Anchor, where Stanley Avenue and Anchor Drive were laid out, serviced with mains water from the start, in 1929–1931. By the end of the 1930s much of Birchwood Avenue had been constructed, although its completion was delayed by the war and it was eventually finished in the 1950s, and there had also been a some minor infill schemes and ribbon

48. Land sales in the area of Hutton village, 1915–22: the break-up of the Rawstorne estate and its division into sale lots was the signal for housing development on an unprecedented scale. Most of the interwar building on both sides of Liverpool Road was made possible by these sales. On this map, for example, lots 1 and 2 of the 1922 sale were the land on which Tolsey Drive was built.

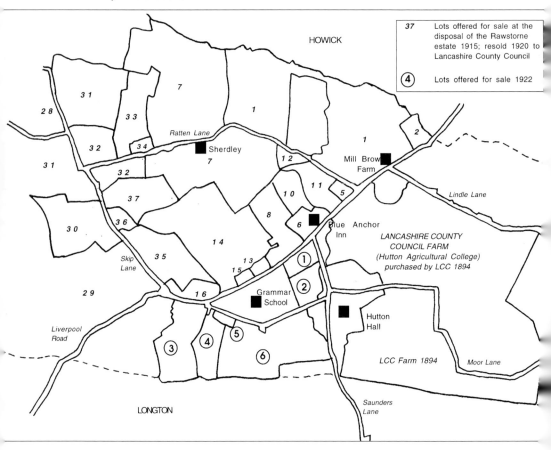

49. Tolsey Drive, which was developed on land sold for building in 1922, was one of the earliest housing schemes in Hutton in the years after the First World War.

development along Liverpool Road. The latter was characteristic of the 1920s and early 1930s, taking advantage of the availability of services at minimum cost, but here ribbon development along classified road front-ages was ended by legislation in 1935.

In 1934 there was another important land sale. The executors of the late A. R. Fish of Holme Mead sold his 164 acre estate at the eastern end of the parish, including the 102 acres of Moor Farm. The description noted that the farm was in an excellent state, had been improved at considerable expense since 1918, and had new farm buildings erected in 1924–1925, 'well known as one of the finest ranges of farm buildings in the country. All the land is in exceptionally good heart and condition and well-drained. The late Mr. Fish spent large sums each year in draining and he was, shortly before his death, of opinion that the drainage of the land was as near perfect as it could be'. Nonetheless, the vendors also encouraged the building trade, pointing out that 'the premises have good frontages to Lindle Lane, Pope Lane, Workhouse Lane and Green Lane, and comprise many excellent sites for the erection of good class residential property': the smaller lots close to Workhouse Lane were described simply as 'valuable building land'. Much of this land was in fact acquired by the County Council and became part of the agricultural college and the police headquarters, but otherwise it is certain that extensive housing development would have taken place in 1935–1939 and from the late 1940s onwards. It is probably the case that although the

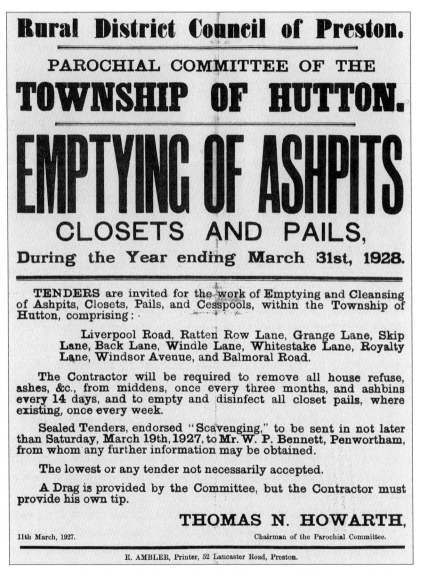

Rural District Council of Preston.

PAROCHIAL COMMITTEE OF THE

TOWNSHIP OF HUTTON.

EMPTYING OF ASHPITS

CLOSETS AND PAILS,

During the Year ending March 31st, 1928.

TENDERS are invited for the work of Emptying and Cleansing of Ashpits, Closets, Pails, and Cesspools, within the Township of Hutton, comprising:—

Liverpool Road, Ratten Row Lane, Grange Lane, Skip Lane, Back Lane, Windle Lane, Whitestake Lane, Royalty Lane, Windsor Avenue, and Balmoral Road.

The Contractor will be required to remove all house refuse, ashes, &c., from middens, once every three months, and ashbins every 14 days, and to empty and disinfect all closet pails, where existing, once every week.

Sealed Tenders, endorsed "Scavenging," to be sent in not later than Saturday, March 19th, 1927, to Mr. W. P. Bennett, Penwortham, from whom any further information may be obtained.

The lowest or any tender not necessarily accepted.

A Drag is provided by the Committee, but the Contractor must provide his own tip.

THOMAS N. HOWARTH,

11th March, 1927.   Chairman of the Parochial Committee.

E. AMBLER, Printer, 52 Lancaster Road, Preston.

50. Scavenging (i.e. refuse collection) was introduced in Hutton parish in 1927, under the auspices of Preston Rural District Council. This poster (LRO PR5014 acc 5616) dates from the spring of 1927, when the contract for the new service was being offered for tender.

intervention of the county, with its college, police headquarters and smallholdings, had a profound effect upon Hutton, it delayed and ultimately prevented the likelihood of very large-scale residential development in the parish. Without the influence of Lancashire County Council, Hutton would certainly be a very different place today.[113]

These new developments increased the pressure for a full range of local services to be provided by the district council. A Hutton parochial committee, comprising representatives of the parish and district, was created in 1923 to administer local matters, and this began to make improvements, but progress was slow and cost implications always held up the decision-making. During the early 1920s the question of fire cover was frequently aired, and the parish was among those which pressed successfully for the opening of the fire station at Lower Penwortham. In 1938 seven acres of land were acquired for the playing fields, which were eventually laid out after the Second World War. The development of Tolsey Drive, the first new estate in the parish, led to the extension of electricity mains from Penwortham, which had been the outer limit of supply by the Preston Electricity Company, and in 1924 the Medical Officer of Health noted that with the imminent provision of gas and electricity in the area conditions would be ripe for a substantial amount of house-building. Scavenging and refuse collection services were instituted by the rural district council in 1927. But the proposed sewerage scheme remained highly contentious. The inadequacy of sanitation in Hutton was a matter of growing concern, and reports of pollution by overflow from cesspools and soakaways became more common during the 1920s – one particular problem was said to be that householders usually emptied the contents of their pail closets directly into roadside ditches. A survey of the parish undertaken in April 1934 recorded a variety of problems including flooded ditches in the Liverpool road area (flooding has been a persistent problem in the Tolsey Drive area for seventy-five years) and the presence of quantities of untreated sewage in watercourses and ditches.[114]

Preston Rural District Council spent years planning the proposed Longton and Penwortham sewerage scheme, but no action was taken because of the large capital cost, a problem of particular significance after 1929 when public finance restrictions began to bite. The parish council wrote to the district council in September 1930 strongly supporting the project, and the Medical Officer of Health reported the problem

51. Anchor Drive and other housing developments on or close to Liverpool Road were built in the 1920s and 1930s on small parcels of land which had been sold for speculative building in 1919 and 1922.

in his annual reports and other submissions, but many residents were not of the same mind: a meeting of Hutton ratepayers held in July 1931 voted overwhelmingly against the sewerage proposals because the rates would have to be increased to pay for the work.[115] In 1933 the district council prepared a revised scheme, to cost £93,000, after the government had turned down its earlier plans, but the ministry once again rejected the idea. The Medical Officer of Health noted sourly that the position, apart from the expenditure of a lot of money on wasted design work, was exactly as it had been twenty years before. The district council again reduced the scale of the project, again met with government rejection, and in the autumn of 1934 decided to abandon all plans for the foreseeable future. In one of his last reports Charles Trimble, the MOH, described the 'deplorable conditions as regards sewage disposal in this area [Hutton and Longton] … at present nothing comes between the houses and the cottages and the roadside ditches and small streams except small septic tanks … the urbanisation and industrial development in rural areas call for a modern system of sewerage'. In the same year, 1938, public opinion

52. As Hutton evolved into a more substantial village it acquired a range of facilities and services. One of the first of these was the Post Office and village shop. The old thatched post office in Hutton Row is shown in this view taken in about 1905.

seems to have moved towards the provision of a proper sewerage scheme, despite the inevitable costs: a petition signed by many local residents complained of the 'objectionable conditions produced by allowing sewage to flow untreated into a watercourse and adjacent ditches'. The war prevented any further progress, and it was not until 1949–51 that the Longton sewerage scheme finally brought modern sanitation to the houses and cottages of Hutton.[116]

After the Second World War the years of austerity and restrictions upon private speculative building meant that residential development did not get under way again until the mid-1950s, but by that time the sewerage scheme had been completed and it became possible to contemplate larger scale building projects. Hutton grew rapidly during the 1950s and this is reflected in the population figures: in 1951 there were 1,388 people and 386 houses, but by 1961, mainly as a result of housing construction around Liverpool Road, there were 1,720 people (an increase of 23%) and 495 dwellings. This rate of growth was unprecedented, greater than 21% increase at the time of the handloom-weaving 'boom'

in the early nineteenth century, but even it paled into relative insignifi-
cance compared with the expansion of Hutton during the 1960s. Between
1961 and 1971 a population increase of 1,097, to a total of 2,817 people
in 885 houses, was recorded. This was a growth rate of no less than
63% in ten years, by far the largest rate of increase in the entire history
of the parish and one which transformed Hutton. During this period
and into the early 1970s several large new estates (notably the Stiles
Avenue – Greenway and Fensway – Greenacres developments) were
constructed on the land which in the 1920s and 1930s was being marketed
as 'eminently suitable' for speculative building. There were also smaller
infilling schemes and some new housing was constructed in the Royalty
Lane area, but the main focus was the village centre, which expanded
considerably and was 'rounded off' in shape. The new housing was
almost entirely occupied by incomers, part of that process noted earlier
whereby the car and the commuting which it allowed altered the living
patterns of so many people and changed the fortunes of places such as
Hutton which lay beyond, but conveniently near, a large commercial
and industrial town.

After the mid-1970s the supply of readily-available new building land
was reduced, partly because of planning constraints. The 1981 population,
indeed, was significantly lower than that of 1971 – a 12% fall, to 2,475,
was recorded. Some of this may be explained by fluctuations in student
numbers at the agricultural college, but in addition the households
established in the 1950s, which originally included small children, had
now come to maturity, the children had moved elsewhere, and there
was a higher proportion of one or two person households. The 1991
figures show a further decrease, almost certainly for the same reason –
Hutton in that census year had 2,148 people, in 833 households. These
figures may be contrasted with the experience of Penwortham and
Farington, both of which showed a continuing large increase in population because of the new housing areas in the Central Lancashire New
Town scheme, and may be compared with the reductions in population
at Longton, Little Hoole and Much Hoole, where circumstances were
not dissimilar to those found in Hutton. Nevertheless, the overall growth
in the fifty years after World War Two is striking – at the end of the
century the population of Hutton was about 60% greater than it had
been in the late 1940s.

29. The Later History of
the Agricultural College

The Agricultural College, opened at Hutton in 1894, quickly established
an enviable reputation for the quality of its teaching and instruction,
and the progressive character of its facilities. With the enthusiastic support
of the Lancashire County Council Education Committee the College
widened the range of its activtities during the years before the First
World War, allowing non-Lancashire students to enroll and developing
a thriving farming enterprise which was – in the early years at least –
commercially successful as well as educationally impressive. New facilities

53. The Home Farm buildings, part of Lancashire Agricultural College at Hutton, in 1975.

included a dairy, purpose-built to the most modern standards (1913), and in the same year a hostel for female students, carefully designed so that nobody from outside could look into the rooms, and the girls could not see out (though high furniture was usually adapted to overcome that difficulty!). A great pride was taken in the College, and in ensuring that everything was maintained to the highest possible standards. Students were kept under a strict regime – one recalled that in the early 1930s 'most students were hard up and of course there was no drinking or staying out late. Jenny Borrett [the matron] gave one permission for an evening out with strict instuctions to be in by 10 p.m. If you were a few minutes late, you would be met on the dorrstep and your escort admonished for keeping you out late. Another simple pleasure for us students was to hold a midnight feast, after receiving a tuck box from home'.

By 1939 the College had 18 full-time and two part-time members of

54. Feeding the beef cattle at the Gables Farm buildings of the Agricultural College, 1975.

staff, and a men's hostel had been built. In that year there were 37 men and 26 women students. During the 1930s there had been several major developments, including a new 'scientific' milking parlour and the rapid expansion of the College's poultry courses, for which in 1937 an experimental battery unit was built: about 10,000 chickens per annum were reared and sold by the late 1930s. There were 260 acres of land, about 50 acres normally being under arable cultivation, and the College had a herd of about 80 non-pedigree cows as well as sheep and pigs. Although horses were still used for much of the farmwork, tractors and other forms of mechanisation were beginning to appear, since as usual the College was determined to maintain its repuutation as a progressive and up-to-date establishment. During the Second World War, however, the normal teaching work of the College was suspended, and after 1945 the Government initiated a series of changes to agricultural education across the country as a whole, pressing for major revision of the type of training offered and the number and size of institutions in this sector of education. Dairying was increasingly centred in large factories and industrial-scale units, so that the farmhouse methods taught at Hutton were becoming irrelevant to modern conditions, while in contrast horticulture, market-gardening and poultry-farming were assuming a greater importance. In 1947 the County Council bought the Winmarleigh Hall estate near Garstang as the site for its new Institute of Agriculture, and teaching began to focus on national diplomas and other qualifications. At Hutton new methods of dairying and poultry courses were the mainstay during the 1950s and early 1960s, but the Institute at Winmarleigh was the base for many of the County's full-time agricultural courses. Although development of the facilities at Hutton continued into the early 1980s, a succession of reports suggested that its scope for future expansion was limited. Similar doubts were expressed about Winmarleigh, which for different reasons was less than ideal, and in 1957 the Ministry of Agriculture, in an inspection report, suggested that the best solution would be to combine all the county's agricultural training and teaching on a single site. With this in mind, the County Council bought the 530 acre Myerscough estate in 1962 and began to develop it as the main centre. There was heavy investment in new buildings, residential accommodation, farm facilities and landscaping and in the late 1980s the decision was taken to carry this process to its logical conclusion – the closure of Hutton and Winmarleigh and the concentration of all operations at Myerscough. This was further encouraged by the ending of the formal control by the County Council in April 1993, when the Lancashire College of Agriculture and Horticulture became a corporate body and was renamed Myerscough College. From this time Hutton, almost precisely a century old, was merely an annexe to the main site.[117]

30. *The New Roads, 1930–2000*

During the inter-war period the rapid growth in private motoring as well as in the motor transport of goods began to produce serious traffic congestion in many places on Lancashire's road network, and as traffic volumes and speeds grew the inadequacy of the existing road network

55. The *Anchor Inn* photographed in about 1925. There had been an inn here since at least the mid-eighteenth century and probably for many decades before that time: from 1770 when the main road became a turnpike the *Anchor* was a well-known landmark *en route*. After the First World War, and the growth of motor traffic, the inn was a favourite destination for people coming out from Preston as well as for coach and charabanc parties on the old main road from Liverpool to Preston and Blackpool.

Call at the Prettiest Filling Station in Great Britain

All Grades of
Petrol.

::

"Duchy"
Motor Oils.

::

Tyres and
Accessories.

::

Free Air and
Water.

Luxuriously
Appointed
Cloak
Rooms
and
Conveniences

DUCHY SERVICE STATION
HUTTON, NEAR PRESTON

On the Main Liverpool—Southport—Preston Road.   Three Miles from Preston.

56. The Duchy Service Station, which has recently closed, was almost a tourist attraction in its own right, and was widely advertised in the local newspapers in the years between the wars.

was increasingly obvious. By the mid-1920s new road construction and the upgrading of existing routes had become a main theme in Lancashire County Council thinking, and the new Ministry of Transport started to make grants for the construction of road improvements or entirely new stretches of main road. Lancashire was early in the field of new road-building and in the late 1920s bypasses were built at, among other places, Garstang and Great Eccleston. The A59, which although not an 'industrial' road carried a very heavy traffic north from Liverpool, was particularly unsatisfactory, its alignment being winding and narrow and the character of the road little altered from pre-turnpike days. In 1922 a bypass was built at Ormskirk and in 1933–37 the major upgrading of the Maghull and Aughton stretches, with wide dual-carriageways, cycle lanes and residential service roads, was implemented. North of the Douglas the difficult length from the river at Bank Hall to Longton was improved in 1925–1926 with short bypasses at Walmer Bridge, Much Hoole and Little Hoole. The largest single project on the northern stretch of the road was to be a bypass for Longton, scheduled to begin in the autumn of 1939. The scheme was associated with the upgrading of the road from the Anchor at Hutton into Penwortham itself, and in 1936–1939 this was carried out. Liverpool Road in Penwortham was

57. *The Anchor* was largely rebuilt in the 1930s to cater for the new trade brought by cars and charabancs. It has since been remodelled and extended several times, but is still a prominent landmark at the entrance to the village.

58. Saunders Lane in about 1930. This country lane, with its attractive area of fine trees and woodland, and with the Hutton Hall estate on the east side, became a popular place for picnics in the 1920s and 1930s, used by Preston people having a Sunday outing and by travellers on the nearby main road from Liverpool. In 1937–39 the northern end was altered by the construction of the new dual-carriageway from the *Anchor* to Howick Cross, and in 1956–57 the Longton bypass was built along the alignment of the northern end of the lane, destroying its rural seclusion for ever.

widened, taking advantage of the broad grassed verges which remained from the seventeenth- and eighteenth-century crofts which lay alongside the old road, while the stretch from Howick Cross to Hutton was made a dual carriageway. This section of the project is now of historical interest, for the design incorporated the most up-to-date and – in retrospect – lavish specifications of the 1930s. There were cycle lanes and footpaths, but most striking is the central reservation. The southern (Hutton-bound) carriageway was constructed within the curtilage of the old Hutton Hall estate, bought by the county in 1937, and the central reservation was built to an exceptional width to allow the preservation of some of the fine old trees along the edge of the estate – Hutton Parish Council had written to the County Surveyor in March 1936 requesting that 'as many trees as possible may be saved in Saunders Lane' when the new road went ahead.[118] This has given this section of trunk road, now seventy years old, a visual quality and interest which its continuation, the later Longton bypass, lacks.

The next stage of the project, the Longton bypass itself, had originally been intended to run from the Anchor, around the south side of Hutton and Longton to meet the A59 north of Walmer Bridge, but by 1938 the County Council was actively considering the building of a motorway network and putting forward schemes to the Ministry for the route which would become the M6. The Second World War put an end to such plans, but in 1949 they were resurrected as the *Road Plan for Lancashire*, a highly influential document which proposed a strategy of massive investment in large-scale road-building, with a comprehensive motorway network supported by upgraded trunk and main roads. One of the motorway routes, the Preston Southern Bypass, would run from the north-south motorway at Walton Summit, via Farington and Ulnes Walton, to the proposed Longton bypass at Hutton, the location of the junction being just south of the police headquarters. Because of this motorway connection the Longton bypass itself would be more important than previously anticipated and a new route, taking the road direct to the southern end of Walmer Bridge, was indicated on the map in the 1949 plan. The bypass itself was regarded as the highest priority and work began in July 1956. It was the first bypass built in the county after the war, and the design reflected the changes in attitude to road construction in the twenty years since the previous designs were prepared. Separate cycle tracks were replaced by a wide footpath and cycleway,

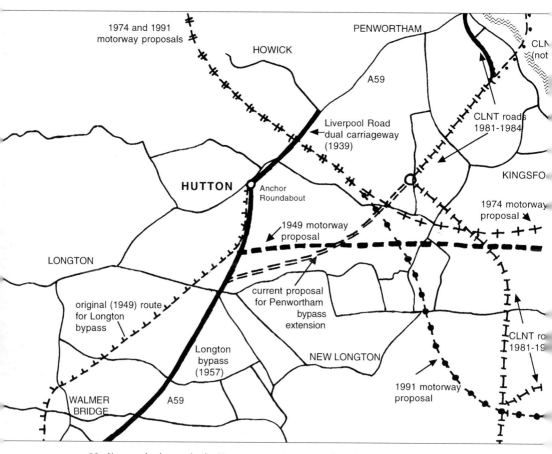

59. New road schemes in the Hutton area, 1930–2000: the criss-crossing of routes proposed or built emphasises the way in which the district was seen as a major corridor for new highways for over seventy years.

but the carriageways for motor vehicles were much wider than the 1930s' plan had proposed. The bypass was opened in December 1957 and in 1973 the junction at Chapel Lane, the scene of numerous serious accidents, was altered by an underpass constructed beneath the bridge of the disused West Lancashire Railway.[119]

The building of the Longton bypass and its associated road schemes had a profound effect on Hutton. The landscape in the vicinity of the Anchor and Ratten Row was altered for ever, with a large new roundabout and the dual carriageways heading towards Penwortham and Walmer Bridge, but the stretch of Liverpool Road between the Anchor and Longton in contrast became a minor road and was relieved of its heavy

60. The fine trees in the central reservation of the dual carriageway east of the *Anchor* are the surviving portions of the plantation woodlands which formerly bordered the Hutton Hall estate.

burden of through traffic. Most of Hutton was bypassed, even if some of the parish received the unwelcome effects of major road construction. We may be grateful, though, that in the 1930s and again in the 1950s considerable efforts were made to ensure that the some of the fine trees and strips of woodland which were characteristic of the Hutton Hall estate were preserved. The approaches to Hutton roundabout, both from the Preston direction and from the Longton bypass, have a parkland quality which – for a busy dual-carriageway – is unexpectedly attractive. Since these two major road schemes were built traffic has of course increased enormously. Their construction, and the upgrading of the Southport and Liverpool roads, has helped to account for the rapid growth of commuting from the Hutton direction into Preston, and long lines of stationary vehicles heading into town are a regular feature of the morning rush-hour, sometimes stretching back from Guild Way for over two miles to Hutton roundabout.

The continuing debate about road-building has a special relevance to Hutton, for the construction in the late 1980s of the first stage of the Penwortham bypass, along the old railway to the edge of the built-up area, was seen as the first stage in a more comprehensive road strategy for South Ribble. In the 1974 outline plan for the Central Lancashire New Town the road network was to be based on a new motorway from the direction of Blackburn and the Calder Valley, via the M6 at Higher Walton and then passing north of Bamber Bridge and on to Howick before crossing the river and joining the M55 near Bartle. At Nutters Platt it was to meet, in a huge interchange, a motorway running south-west towards Liverpool, paralleling the A59. At this interchange a new dual carriageway would also join, coming from central Preston through Penwortham and then linking up with the Longton bypass near Chapel Lane. The New Town designated area did not include Hutton, but it could have had a dramatic impact upon the parish. The 1974 proposals clearly incorporated several of the key elements from the 1949 plan, including the Preston-Liverpool motorway and the Preston Southern Bypass, but although some routes in the 1974 plan were built, the motorway sections were still on the drawing board when the New Town scheme faded away in the early 1980s.[120]

However, in 1991 the government announced that the Preston Southern and Western Bypass, a six-lane motorway, was to be constructed from the M6 at Bamber Bridge, via Howick and the Ribble bridge, to join the M55. The proposed new road aroused very widespread and vociferous local opposition, because most of the remaining open land between Howick and Hutton was destined to disappear, and it would thus have had a massive impact upon the surviving rural landscape as well as on the urban and suburban areas on either side. Associated with the motorway scheme was the extension of the Penwortham bypass to join the A59 in the vicinity of Hutton, a road which, as already noted, had been in highway plans since at least 1949. Hutton Parish Council conducted a survey of opinion within the parish in the autumn of 1991, shortly after plans for the two linked road schemes were made public. The survey revealed that 79% of respondents were opposed to the motorway and 54% to the bypass extension, and so the council's initial response was to register opposition to both projects.[121] Two years later, as government road-building plans were drastically scaled down across the country as a whole, the Preston Southern and Western Bypass was dropped from the roads programme, but the bypass scheme remained and the County Council began consultation and preliminary planning procedures. Two routes were put forward. One (the Brown Route) linked the roundabout at Broad Oak to the present A59 adjacent to Howick School. The other (the Blue Route) followed a longer alignment from the end of the existing road, past New Longton, to the A59 south of the police headquarters. Locally the choice between the two routes caused heated argument and high-profile campaigns were fought by the supporters and opponents of both. The parish council, mindful that the Howick route might have a very damaging impact upon the school and would also funnel the traffic back onto the A59 before the Anchor roundabout, came down, on balance, in favour of the original New Longton route, as did many Hutton residents. In 1998 the 'Blue' route, from Broad Oak to the Longton bypass, was selected by the County Council but there the matter rests, and in May 2000 it was suggested that the project had been deferred for at least another decade.

31. *Hutton Since 1975: Challenges and the Community*

The possibility of large-scale housing development caused considerable disquiet in the parish during the 1980s and 1990s. Hutton was outside the boundary of the New Town, so there was no general presumption of the planning authorities in favour of growth, but as an attractive and conveniently located semi-rural area it naturally came within the gaze of property developers. In the late 1960s the extension of the Longton sewerage scheme to the land between Sherdleys, Skip Lane and Liverpool Road connected most of the remaining unsewered properties in the parish and also opened up the possibility of development north of Liverpool Road. When considering its response to the County Structure Plan proposals in 1979 the parish council urged that efforts should be made 'to prevent an unacceptable demand for suburban rural residential accommodation',[122] and from this time onwards there was stronger resistance to the idea of development. Hutton was then – and still is – substantially protected by the 'green belt' and the central area of the

61. Hutton Manor (formerly Mayor's Farm): there are relatively few old buildings in Hutton, and most of the housing dates from the early 1920s onwards. The surviving earlier buildings are therefore a valuable link with the past.

village bordering on Liverpool Road provided the only area potentially available for housing development. In January 1984 the parish council underlined their position, stating to the borough council that future development within the village should be restricted essentially to sheltered accommodation to meet local needs on the former School House site, opposite to the grammar school entrance. It also suggested that, if as seemed likely, many of the police houses in Lindle Lane became surplus to requirements, they would provide a valuable opportunity to increase the stock of affordable housing for local people.[123]

However, in the spring of that year the borough council published their draft Western Parishes Local Plan, covering Hutton, Longton, Much Hoole and Little Hoole. This included proposed provision for new housing land to be released in Hutton and Longton. In response, the parish council registered strong opposition to the proposal, which involved the designation of 11 acres of land to the north of Liverpool Road, adjacent to The Greenacres, for hosung development. It was argued that the possibility of up to 100 additional houses would radically alter the balance between developed and undeveloped land in Hutton, greatly increasing its population and damaging the still-rural character of this part of the village. The council pointed out that the major developments of the previous thirty years – such as Anchor Drive and Stiles Avenue – had been absorbed without serious detriment to that character, but that the new proposal would be excessive. Its own housing survey, conducted during April 1986, found little local demand for housing except for a small number of sheltered units. Few local people wanted more 'executive' homes to be built, and the only demand for new developments in the parish would apparently come from outsiders. These pressures, it was felt, could be better catered for elsewhere. The survey showed that 91% of the properties in Hutton were owner-occupied, but that 50% of households had only one or two people and 11% of households were comprised of retired people over 70 years of age. In the final version of the Local Plan, approved in 1987, the proposed housing west of The Greenacres was deleted and the Borough Council withdrew the possibility of large-scale development in this part of the parish.

This decision was widely welcomed throughout the village. However, local plans have a currency of only ten years and the attraction of the location to developers remained. It was perhaps not surprising, therefore, that the successor South Ribble Local Plan, issued for consultation in June 1994, again proposed the release of land for housing development. This time, moreover, the whole area within the 'green belt' fence, totalling 23 acres (twice the scale envisaged in 1984) was earmarked for 200 homes, including a quota for 'affordable' properties. The potential impact on the village of this scale of development was huge and resisting the proposal presented a very real challenge ot the community. Local reaction was strong and the parish council invested considerable energy and funds in ensuring, through their planning consultant, that Hutton's case was well-represented to the public inquiry in spring 1996. The weight of objection was significantly augmented by that of other local objectors, a number of whom collaborated with the parish council.

A long wait ensued before the inspector's report was finally published in September 1998 and it was with great relief that, in the event, Hutton's arguments prevailed and the threat of large-scale development was removed. In planning terms, the Local Plan, formally adopted by the borough council in February 2000, now implies a general presumption against development which should be helpful in the longer term. Happily, at the same time, the potential remains for a small-scale sheltered development to meet community needs.[124] Despite expectations of such a development having first emerged as far back as 1986, past efforts to bring a sheltered scheme to Hutton have not yet proved successful.

By this time, though, another potential site for large-scale development had emerged. In March 1997 the first formal notification of the impending closure of the agricultural college was received, although the possibility had been aired for some years before. Reorganisation of further education meant that in 1993 the Lancashire College of Agriculture became an independent and self-governing institution, taken out of the control of the County Council. It began a programme of rationalisation, with the aim of concentrating its activities at the Myerscough Campus, and the closure of the Hutton site thus became a priority. In the autumn of 1999 the site was offered for sale, and in May 2000 planning consent was sought for the demolition of all the existing buildings and the constructuion of a complex of 63 new homes. This is a significant development for the village and its history. The college will however maintain its links with Hutton as farming activities are to continue on the surrounding land, centred on Gables Farm, for the foreseeable future.[125]

The development of new housing in the eastern part of the parish, adjacent to New Longton, continued in the late 1970s and early 1980s, especially in Windsor Avenue, Balmoral Road and Royalty Avenue, which were accessible only from New Longton and had no direct road connection with the rest of Hutton. In 1983 the Department of the Environment started a comprehensive review of parish boundaries in the Borough of South Ribble, following preliminary notification in 1977. In its submission to the borough council, Hutton Parish Council suggested alterations to the boundary with Longton which would, it felt, produce a more logical and effective unit – these were the transfer of the Windsor

Avenue and Balmoral Road area from Hutton to Longton, and likewise
the properties at the north end of Shirley Lane. As is often the case in
such exercises, there were counter-proposals. Among these was a suggestion in 1979 by Longton Parish Council that Hutton parish should be
abolished and its entire area included within Longton, on the grounds
that there was no discernible community feeling in Hutton and that its
focus and interests lay with Longton. Hutton Parish Council had naturally opposed this suggestion vigorously, arguing that 'Hutton is a distinct
and viable community with an identity of its own',[126] and in 1983
Longton modified its position, proposing instead that the eastern half
of Hutton beyond the disused West Lancashire Railway line and including the Pope Lane area, should be added to Longton. This plan was
rejected by the borough council before it made its submission to the
Government, and the borough preferred instead the modest changes put
forward by Hutton. These came into effect in March 1987.

As the population of Hutton grew, and it became a substantial community, the range of facilities required to serve its population also
increased. The development of basic services, which had begun with the
introduction of scavenging and refuse-collection in 1927, was completed
in 1966–67 when most of the residential areas of the parish were provided
with street-lighting. By the mid-1970s, however, new concerns were being
expressed, about the state of the local environment and the need for
community facilities. In the past Hutton, a small and scattered community, did not have a powerful sense of its own identity but the influx
of new residents may have helped to develop that feeling. In the spring
of 1980 the parish council began to publish a regular news sheet, the
Hutton News, which contained details of its activities and of current
issue affecting the parish. Thus, the first *Hutton News* reported on the
annual parish meeting; the need for a village hall; library facilities, the
mobile library service having been withdrawn on the opening of the
new Longton Library; the litter problem; speeding on Liverpool Road;
difficulties with bus services; stray dogs, seats and footpaths; and Longton
Parish Council's proposals that Hutton and Longton should amalgamate
as a single parish.

Fuelling the increase in community feeling was the proliferation of
local societies and clubs, which helped to cement the new identity of
the parish.[127] One of the first was the Tennis Club, founded in 1962,
but in the 1980s many others followed – the Hutton Garden Club was

founded in October 1980 and others including the Hutton Toddler Group, the Hutton Ladies Group, the Village Playgroup, the Art Club, the Shotokan Karate Club, the Local History and Interest Society, and the Walking Club. That all these flourish provides convincing evidence of the growth of identity in the parish, but perhaps the most important community activity during the 1980s was the construction of the village hall. Without this facility most of the organisations mentioned could not have started, and indeed many were set up in anticipation of the new hall, with the Grammar School accommodating their early meetings under arrangements negotiated by the parish council. During the 1970s local people had been increasingly aware that Hutton had no convenient meeting place for groups and activities – the Garden Club, for example, was forced initially to meet at Longton Library – and the suggestion that facilities at the grammar school could 'double up' for community use met with little support from the governors at that time. The parish council took the matter in hand and a parish meeting held in January 1981 expressed strong support for the project. In May 1981 a Hutton Village Hall Association was formed to raise money for the work, and all sorts of fundraising activities and community events which heightened awareness of the project were held, such as coach trips, concerts, dances, village parties, Halloween bonfires and jumble sales.

The level of local involvement was very high and the fundraising campaign itself had an important spin-off in emphasising community identity. Substantial funding contributions were obtained from the county, borough and parish councils, and although there were many setbacks work began in the summer of 1985 and the hall was opened by Robert Atkins, MP for South Ribble, in May 1986. An extension, providing a stage, was opened in the spring of 1990 – as before, the fundraising was by voluntary effort and a packed programme of events and activities – and in 1997 a second extension, with storeroom, bar and improved toilets, was added. Today, the hall has become the central feature of Hutton's flourishing community life and provides an excellent meeting place for the many groups and clubs within the parish. A central feature of early fundraising for the village hall was the establishment of the annual village fete, held on the May Day Bank Holiday Monday. This grew in size over the ten years or so following the opening of the hall, and a very considerable involvement from across the community developed. The fete continues to thrive in the new century, as na important local event and one which attracts large crowds from Hutton and the wider area, raising valuable revenue ot support the upkeep of the village hall.

During the past thirty years continuing efforts have been made by the parish council and local groups to maintain and enhance the environment of the village. Such an attitude was not entirely new, for in the mid-1930s, when the Liverpool road was lined with hoardings, the parish council commented on the 'unsightly advertising boards' in the vicinity of the Anchor and asked the district and county councils to 'endeavour to preserve the amenities of the District relative to Hutton Hall', which was 'being spoiled by picnickers' who partially blocked Saunders Lane with their cars every Sunday.[128] Much more recently there has been a growing awareness of the need for proper care of footpaths, in the rural parts of the parish as well as the built-up area, and the potential value of these for recreational and leisure purposes has been emphasised by the designation of the Ribble Way, which passes through Hutton, as a long-distance route. The woodland and trees along roads leading into Hutton, including the stands of oaks around Saunders Lane and the Anchor roundabout, have been protected and there is a proper policy for replacing those which are too old. Bulb-planting, providing seats and benches, maintaining the duck pond and upgrading the playing fields are all matters which have been given attention, and the parish council has encouraged action on a variety of other environmental issues, while the children's play area has been refurbished for summer 2000 under an joint initiative between the borough and parish councils.

32. *The Future*

Hutton will not stay as it is, for change is an ever-present feature of any community. Over the past half-century the parish has altered at an unprecedented rate, as new roads have been built, housing developments have taken place, and the population has not only increased rapidly but has changed in its composition and character. Like so many other communities close to large towns and on main traffic routes, there are all sorts of pressures which must be accommodated or resisted, many of these forces for change being those over which local people have little direct control. But, as this book has shown, there has never been a time when some change was not evident. The landscape of Hutton was being radically altered in the seventeenth and eighteenth centuries, and no doubt some people then regretted the loss of familiar landmarks, lamented the disappearance of everyday sights and sounds, and wondered what the future would bring. One of the other themes of this book, though, is that today we are more aware than ever before of our heritage. That is a much over-used word, but collective consciousness of the inherited landscape, of local history, of natural history and ecology, and of the value and quality of these aspects of the community, has never been greater. In the half-century from the end of the 1920s much that was attractive and of considerable intrinsic interest in Hutton was lost, but today people are more prepared to fight to keep what is valued. Likewise, the sense of community in Hutton has grown apace, perhaps in part because of all those changes. The thriving clubs and societies, the community action and events, the willingeness of local people to voice their concerns about planning issues, and the awareness of amenity and environment, are all positive forms of change. Let us hope that, in the coming decades, the changes which will undoubtedly take place in Hutton will harmonise with its landscape, respect its historic past, and merge unobtrusively with the community of the present.

Appendix: List of the Tenants[129] *of the Manor of Hutton, 1720*

Matthew Farrar	J Stevenson	Robert Mair lawyer
William Marton	R Bamber junior	Robert Mair senior
Hugh Waring	George Pert	J Mair Nellys
George Ridley	Richard Mair	Robert Mair junior
John Forshaw	William Moss	Ellen Bickerstaffe
Robert Wilding	J Stevenson junior	Peter Walch
John Martin	Edward Short	Ralph Southworth
John Martin junior	Evan Maudsley	Edward Mair
Widow Cawdrey	R Bamber senior	Robert Moss
Widow Kester	Widow Wilding	Roger Charnley
Thomas Farrar	Evan Procter	William Wilkins
Edward Mawdsley	William Clayton	William Loxham
Thomas Mair	John Taylor	George Birchall
Widow Wilkins	William Beardsworth	Thomas Mair jun, son of Robert
Thomas Harrison	William Bibby	George Tuson
Mr Thomas Whalley	Thomas Dimmock	Robert Rutter
William Bamber	Widow Cliffe	John Smith
Henry Mair	son of widow Cliffe	Henry Mair
Richard Forrest	J Mair son of George	Christopher Bibby
Widow Miller	John Brewer	Mr Thomas Loxham

Notes and References

1. These investigations were undertaken as part of the North West Wetlands Survey.
2. See M. Gelling, *Place-names in the landscape* (Dent, 1984, pp. 167–9, for a discussion of *hoh* place-names.
3. For more information about the Domesday entry for Penwortham, and a background discussion, see A. G. Crosby, *Penwortham in the Past* (Carnegie, 1988), pp. 19–22.
4. See A. G. Crosby, *Penwortham in the Past* (1988), pp. 23–7 for a full account of Penwortham church and the organisation of its parish in the medieval and early modern periods.
5. More information about Longton chapel is given in Marjorie Searson, *Longton: A Village History* (Carnegie, 1988), pp. 34–5.
6. The Premonstratensians, known from their habits as the 'white canons', were a lesser order, founded in 1121, at Premontre near Laon, France, by St Norbert. They followed the Augustinian rule but were organised on the same lines as the Cistercians, choosing remote sites and developing as large-scale landowners and estate managers. There were 38 houses of the order in England.
7. A version of the Cockersand Cartulary, much the most important source for the medieval history of Hutton (and among the key documents for medieval Lancashire), was published a century ago in Latin with English summaries William Farrer (ed.), *The Chartulary of Cockersand Abbey of the Premonstratensian Order*, in seven parts, Chetham Society, New Series, volumes 38 (1898), 39 (1898), 40 (1898), 43 (1900), 56 (1905), 57 (1905) and 64 (1909). Page references to the cartulary below are for this edition, which is paginated continuously through the seven volumes. *Cockersand Cartulary*, pp. 392–3.
8. *Cockersand Cartulary*, pp. 63 and 292–3.
9. The style of dating 1230 x 1240 indicates that the precise date is unknown but that the event took place sometime between these two years. Because of the uncertainty and unreliability of dating documents in the early medieval period this convenient form is very widely used by historians when only an approximate date can be calculated.
10. *Cockersand Cartulary*, pp. 409–10.
11. *Cockersand Cartulary*, p. 410 (note that the quotation, as in all references to items in the Cockersand Cartulary, is a translation rendered in modern English, since all these documents are written in medieval Latin).
12. *Cockersand Cartulary*, pp. 411–12, 420 and 418.
13. Tithes were the payment of one-tenth of all agricultural and other produce originally intended for the support of the parish clergy, tithes were often transferred to other owners – in this instance, the parish church was itself 'owned' by Evesham and so the abbey took the proceeds. After the Dissolution of the monasteries in the late 1530s their tithe rights passed to lay owners, out of church hands altogether.
14. *Cockersand Cartulary*, pp. 395–6.
15. *Cockersand Cartulary*, pp. 395–9.

16. 'carr' is a dialect term for swampy overgrown ground, or wetland; from the Old Norse, *kjarr*.

17. *Cockersand Cartulary*, pp. 409–10 and 411–12.

18. LRO DDF 524.

19. *Cockersand Cartulary*, pp. 434–5.

20. *Cockersand Cartulary*, pp. 409–10, 411–12, 416 and 446.

21. *Cockersand Cartulary*, p. 423; LRO DDHe 23/25.

22. *Cockersand Cartulary*, p. 1186; the Penwortham Moss turbaries are described in A. G. Crosby, *Penwortham in the Past* (1988), pp. 66–70.

23. LRO DDF 543.

24. A rood or rod was five and a half yards in statute measure and eight yards by Lancashire measure the latter is used in this early seventeenth-century document.

25. LRO DDF 524.

26. *Cockersand Cartulary*, pp. 411–12, 425.

27. The published transcript gives the name as 'Howin-carr', but Howick is probably intended.

28. *Cockersand Cartulary*, pp. 423 and 430.

29. *Cockersand Cartulary*, pp. 442 and 446; for 'rising-bridges' in Lancashire see M. C. Higham, 'The roads of Dark Age and medieval Lancashire', ch. 2 in A. G. Crosby (ed.), *Leading the Way: A History of Lancashire's Roads* (Lancashire County Books, 1998), p. 40.

30. *Cockersand Cartulary*, p. 1254 Bradford Greaves was next to Mill Brook, just downstream of Liverpool Road and about two hundred yards west of the present Howick School.

31. LRO DDF 532.

32. Enclosure was the process of dividing up tracts of open land – grassland, moor or moss – by making boundaries, ditching or hedging, and thus creating fields in the modern sense the land was, at the same time, taken out of communal use and converted to private occupation by an individual farmer or tenant.

33. *Cockersand Cartulary*, p. 1254; LRO DDF 543.

34. LRO DDF 528 and 530.

35. DDHe 23/6, 23/28, 23/26 and 25/79; for Longton, see A. J. L. Winchester, 'Field, wood and forest – landscapes of medieval Lancashire', in A. G. Crosby (ed.), *Lancashire Local Studies in honour of Diana Winterbotham* (Carnegie and Lancashire Local History Federation, 1993), pp. 13–16.

36. *Cockersand Cartulary*, pp. 434–5.

37. *Cockersand Cartulary*, pp. 431–2; for more information on monastic granges in general, see Colin Platt, *The Monastic Grange in Medieval England* (Macmillan, 1969).

38. *Cockersand Cartulary*, pp. 1254 ff.

39. LRO DDF 524.

40. LRO DDF 530.

41. *Cockersand Cartulary*, p. 437.

42. *Cockersand Cartulary*, pp. 395–6 and 428; the term 'waingate' is used in several other deeds of the first half of the thirteenth century.

43. *Cockersand Cartulary*, p. 437.

44. LRO DDF 526.

45. See M. C. Higham, 'The roads of Dark Age and medieval Lancashire', ch. 2 in

A. G. Crosby (ed.), *Leading the Way: A History of Lancashire's Roads* (1998), esp. pp. 31–2. I am indebted to Mary Higham for discussing this name with me.

46. *Cockersand Cartulary*, p. 433.

47. There were several coppiced woodlands, including some with 'grove' names, in Penwortham.

48. *Cockersand Cartulary*, p. 417; LRO DDHe 23/5; LRO DDF 533.

49. *Cockersand Cartulary*, pp. 438, 1212–20, and 440.

50. LRO DDX 557/4/1 and 557/4 (unnumbered); the lying stone was the bottom stone, which did not move, while the running stone was the upper stone, which revolved upon it.

51. More information on the history of the family is given in a useful, though incomplete, typescript account by Brian Denny (1968) copy in the Lancashire Local Studies collection at the Lancashire Record Office; a copy of the letters patent of Henry VIII 1546 is LRO DDX 43/1.

52. LRO WCW Peter Rawsthorne, 1638.

53. *The Diaries of Lawrence Rawstorne 1810–1849* (typescript copy in Lancashire Local Studies collection at Lancashire Record Office).

54. A court leet was the sitting of the manor court at which the regulation of the local community, including the issuing and enforcement of bye-laws, was the main business this usually operated in parallel with the court baron, which dealt with tenancies and the internal administration of the manor itself.

55. LRO QSP 91/22.

56. LRO QSP 35/4.

57. LRO QSP 75/26.

58. LRO QSB 1/233/28.

59. LRO QSP 774/7 and QSP 730/10.

60. LRO QSP 138/13.

61. LRO QSP 178/18; QSP 223/2; QSP 227/16.

62. LRO QSP 207/30.

63. LRO QSP 255/6.

64. LRO QSP 259/1; QSP 271/1.

65. LRO QSP 259/4.

66. LRO QSP 428/9; QSP 452/31; QSP 498/9; QSP 517/22; QSP 550/25.

67. The letter is quoted in Historic Manuscripts Commission Report xiv, *Manuscripts of Lord Kenyon* (1894), p. 193.

68. I am indebted to the Lancashire County Council Environment Directorate and to Dr Peter Iles for giving me access to the Lancashire Sites and Monuments Record entry concerning the Hutton workhouse.

69. *Further Report of the Commissioners for inquiring concerning Charities* (1825), County of Lancaster parish of Penwortham township of Hutton, pp. 194–205 (Hutton Charities).

70. For more information on the early history of the school, see Marjorie Searson, *Longton: A Village History* (1988), pp. 34–8.

71. *Further Report of the Commissioners for inquiring concerning Charities* (1825), County of Lancaster parish of Penwortham township of Hutton, pp. 194–205 (Penwortham Grammar School).

72. For all the wills and probate inventories discussed, the referencing takes the following

form LRO WCW (for the Archdeaconry of Chester), name of testator and year, e.g. WCW John Harrison alias Hughes, 1623.

73. Lancashire County Council and Department of National Heritage, *List of Buildings of Special Architectural or Historic Interest Hutton Parish* (May 1994); and individual site and building sheets kindly made available by the Lancashire Sites and Monuments Record (Lancashire County Council Environment Directorate, 1999).

74. LRO DDX 741/16/7.

75. For more information on this subject, see D. Winterbotham, 'Sackclothes and fustyans and such like com'odyties early linen manufacture in the Manchester region' , chapter 2 in E. Roberts (ed.), *Linen in the North West* (CNWRS, 1998).

76. Comparable changes were under way in other townships within Penwortham parish at this time see A. G. Crosby, *Penwortham in the past* (1988), pp. 85–9.

77. The other marshes of the Ribble had a comparable history, and organised management of the marsh is very well documented on the north bank, opposite Hutton, where the Freckleton and Newton marshes are still subject to communal control. I am most grateful to Peter Shakeshaft of St Anne's for discussing the Ribble marshes with me.

78. The information on the marsh and its management is derived from LRO DDR Box 61, 'Hutton Marsh Callings' (1712–32).

79. 'stinted' means 'managed by allocation of grazing rights'.

80. LRO DDR 5/19.

81. LRO DDF 894.

82. LRO DDF 912.

83. LRO DDX 103 Box 15.

84. LRO DDX 103 Box 55.

85. LRO DDX 103 Box 15.

86. LRO DDX 103 Box 22 and Box 55.

87. We must always bear in mind that such documents might repeat clauses of this sort simply because they had always appeared in leases for that particular property, not because they were relevant to that specific date.

88. LRO DDX 103 Box 55.

89. Diary of Lawrence Rawstorne of Penwortham unpublished typescript in Lancashire Local Studies Collection, Lancashire Record Office (see p. 33 for the statement of income and outgoings, 2 February 1815). Rawstorne's figures may be compared with the income of £4,123, including tithe receipts, for the Hutton estate in 1823 (LRO DDR 5/32).

90. Figures add up to more than 100% because of rounding of percentage totals.

91. See, for example, Marjorie Searson, *Longton: A Village History* (1988), pp. 61–4, 68; A. G. Crosby, *Penwortham in the Past* (1988), pp. 87–9.

92. *Further Report of the Commissioners for Inquiring Concerning Charities County of Lancaster, Parish of Penwortham* (1825), pp. 194–205 Penwortham Grammar School; 15th Report of the Charity Commissioners, 1826, p. 194.

93. Charity Commissioners, *Returns of Endowed Charities for Lancashire with consolidated reports 1853–1894* (1908), pp. 301–2.

94. Hutton Parish Council minutes, 19 May 1976.

95. J. Whiteley, 'The Turnpike Era', chap. 5 in A. G. Crosby (ed.), *Leading the Way: A History of Lancashire's Roads* (1998).

96. See J. Dakres, *The Last Tide: A History of the Port of Preston, 1806–1981* (Carnegie,

1986) chap. 1); information in this section is largely derived from this source and from J. Barron, *The History of the Ribble Navigation* (1938).

97. The information in this section is taken mainly from G. O. Holt, *Regional History of the Railways of Great Britain, vol. X, the North West* (186 edition), pp. 76–9, 103 and 209–10.

98. LRO PR5014, Hutton PC Minutes 1895–1936; 3 April and 28 April 1899; 3 July 1924.

99. Edith Rigby's remarkable life is chronicled in Phoebe Hesketh, *My Aunt Edith* (Lancashire County Books edn, 1989).

100. In 1902, for example, the death rate in Hutton was 9.56/1000 compared with a national rate of 15.3/1000 and a rate for Preston RD of 14.25/1000) (MOH Report, 1902).

101. LRO RDP 17/1, Preston Rural District Council MOH Report, 1899.

102. LRO RDP 17/1 (MOH reports for 1910 and 1913).

103. LRO DDX 74/16/7, *Sale Plan and Catalogue for Hutton and Howick estate 1915*.

104. LRO CC/TIR/1, Report of Director of Technical Instruction 1891, p. 398.

105. LRO CC/TIR/3, Report of Director of Technical Instruction 1893–94, pp. 54–6.

106. LRO CC/TIR/6, Report of Director of Technical Instruction 1896–97.

107. LRO CC/TIS/2/1, Minutes of Farming Sub-Committee, 14 March and 2 May 1894; 20 March 1895.

108. LRO CC/SHM/3, Minutes of Smallholdings Committee (1918–1919) .

109. LRO CC/CHM/1 (1919–20).

110. LRO CC/CHM/2 (1921–22).

111. For a background history of the Lancashire Constabulary see R. Dobson, *Policing in Lancashire 1839–1989* (Landy Books, 1989); the formulation of proposals for the new HQ is minuted in LRO CC/SJM/1 (Police Standing Joint Committee minutes).

112. See LRO CC/SJM/1 (Police Standing Joint Committee minutes) 1939–1946; *Lancashire Constabulary Journal*, vol. 1, no. 7 (January 1959), pp. 13–14 and vol. 2, no. 5 (January 1961), pp. 188–91.

113. LRO DDX 47/16/74.

114. LRO PR5014 Hutton Parish Council minutes, 5 October 1922, 11 January 1923, 19 September 1923, 24 January 1924, 25 April 1927; RDP 17/1 MOH report 1933, p. 21.

115. LRO PR5014 Hutton Parish Council minutes 11 September 1930, 23 July 1931, 18 April 1934.

116. LRO RDP 17/1 MOH report 1933, p. 21; RDP 17/1 MOH report 1933, p. 21; 1937 report, p. 30; 1938 report, p. 32.

117. The information in this section is largely derived from T. Spreckley, *Myerscough College: A Lancashire Centenary* (Myerscough College, 1993); in this short book there is much of relevance to the history of Hutton, including quotations from interviews and letters of former students and members of staff and reminiscences of life at Hutton Agricultural College in the years up to the 1970s.

118. LRO PR5015, Hutton Parish Council minutes, 17 March 1936.

119. For background to this section see J. Whiteley, 'The beginning of the motor age 1880–1940' and H. Yeadon, 'The motorway era', chapters 6 and 7 in A. G. Crosby (ed.), *Leading the Way: A History of Lancashire's Roads* (1998); pages 219–20 and 277–8 refer specifically to the A59 improvements and bypasses.

120. *Central Lancashire Development Corporation Outline Plan* (CLDC 1974), pp. 108–15

(explanation of transport policies) and pp. 146–7 and 160–1 (explanation of the geography of the road proposals).

121. Hutton Parish Council, minutes, 28 November 1991.

122. Hutton Parish Council, minutes, 28 November 1979.

123. Hutton Parish Council, minutes, 26 January 1984.

124. Hutton Parish Council, minutes, 9 May 1985, 30 July 1985 (letter to Borough Council), 25 September 1986], 13 November 1986, 11 January 1996, 12 November 1998 and 23 September 1999.

125. Hutton Parish Council minutes, March 1997 to December 1999 and 18 May 2000, and reports in the *Lancashire Evening Post*, 1997–99.

126. *Hutton News*, no. 1, Spring 1980.

127. Much of the information about Hutton in the 1980s and 1980s is taken from the Parish Council's *Hutton News* (no. 1, Spring 1980, to no. 31 (summer 1998) and from the minutes of the Parish Council.

128. LRO PR5014 Hutton Parish Council minutes 14 April 1930, 16 April 1931, 23 March 1935 and 17 March 1936.

129. LRO DDR box 61, Hutton Marsh Callings 1712–32].

List of Subscribers

NB A dash (—) indicates where subscribers requested anonymity.

1   David, Cath and Kate Sedgwick, Hutton
2   Mr A. Wignall, Hutton
3   D. K. and S. M. Richardson, Hutton
4   Mr and Mrs Henry Sutton, Longton
5   Mr and Mrs P. R. Eaves, Hutton
6   Mr and Mrs Conlon, Draughton, N. Yorks
7   Rob and Sue Adams, Hutton
8   Mr and Mrs W. D. Latham, Hutton
9   Geoffrey N. Garratt, Penwortham
10 John Thomas Wright, Hutton
11 Miss E. Boardman, Hutton
12 John Crook, Hutton
13 H. Duckworth, Hutton
14 Mr and Mrs K. A. James, Hutton
15 Mr and Mrs J. H. Hull, Hutton
16 Stephen Hull, Hutton
17 David Foulkes, Hutton
18 Phillip Artis, Longton
19 Nigel D. Francis, Hutton
20 Delores Ann Senton, Hutton
21 Mr and Mrs Peter Kempster, Hutton
22 Mr and Mrs Smith, Hutton
23 Miss Lucy S. Scott, New Zealand
24 Reg and Kath Alder, Hutton
25 Rev. Canon William Riley, Hutton
26 Mrs Marjorie Doreen Riley, Hutton
27 Mrs T. Fawcett, Much Hoole
28 David, Lesley and James Boston, Hutton

29   Robert Baxter, Hutton
30   Mr and Mrs T. J. Parker, Hutton
31   Ronald J. H. Reader, Hutton
32   L. and G. Atkinson, Hutton
33   Ken and Pam Naylor, Hutton
34   Mrs M. J. Prescott, Hutton
35   A. G. Bracewell, Hutton
36   Mrs Ros Dark, Hutton
37   Mr and Mrs P. Dewhurst, Hutton
38   Mr T. J. and Mrs V. J. Hastewell, Whitestake
39   —
40   Mr and Mrs J. R. Cookson, Hutton
41   John and Renée Rimmer, Hutton
42   Joyce V. Smith, Hutton
43   Mr and Mrs A. Eccles, Hutton
44   Mrs Barbara Williams, Hutton
45   Derek Lester, Hutton
46   Mrs E. M. Harrison, Hutton
47   Andrew Jones, Hutton
48   Mr Jeffrey James Smith, Hutton
49   L. Howarth, Hutton
50   Sylvia and Roger Rymer, Hutton
51   Mrs Evalyn D. Parry, Hutton
52   Mrs Ann Hartley, Hutton
53   The Greenall Family, Hutton
54   Mr and Mrs C. R. Saunders, Hutton
55   Steven Hart, Hutton
56   Mr and Mrs C. G. Harrison, Hutton
57   P. R. and P. Butterworth, Hutton
58   Mr Leslie Butler, Hutton
59   Mrs M. Whitefoot, Hutton
60   Mr E. Dalton, Hutton
61   Mrs J. Harrison, Hutton
62   Kate Poppleton, Hutton
63   R. P. and A. Dowson, Hutton
64   —
65   —
66   —

67	Robert Hamer, Hutton
68	—
69	Mr K. and Mrs J. Yates, Hutton
70	J. A. Wilshere, Hutton
71	David and Kathrine Muir, Hutton
72	Mr and Mrs Wareing, New Longton
73	The Hann Family, Hutton
74	John Harrison, Hutton
75	J. Eastwood, Hutton
76	A. P. Whitworth, Hutton
77	Doreen and Roger Mitchell, Hutton
78	Mr W. M. and Mrs B. E. Crossley, Hutton
79	Mrs J. A. Bradley, Hutton
80	—
81	—
82	Darren Lynch, Hutton
83	Mr and Mrs E. J. Hamer, Hutton
84	Mrs Lorna Turner, Walmer Bridge
85	Mr and Mrs R. Taylor, Hutton
86	George and Irene Kincla, Hutton
87	Barbara Thackeray, Hutton
88	Mrs Joan Bonney, Hutton
89	William Miller, Hutton
90	Anne and Neville Horsfall, Hutton
91	Mr and Mrs T. Wynn, Hutton
92	Mr S. J. Connell, Hutton
93	—
94	—
95	Jean Gabbatt, Hutton
96	Mrs M. Parker, Hutton
97	Mr and Mrs R. S. Thompson, Hutton
98	M. E. Morgan, Whitestake
99	Mr and Mrs S. W. Harrison, Hutton
100	Mabel Lawson, Hutton
101	Mr and Mrs G. Armstrong, Hutton
102	—
103	A. H. and L. Fishwick, Hutton
104	Mr and Mrs W. S. Hiles, Hutton

105 Lynda M. Quinn, Hutton

106 Beryl Clark, Hutton

107 Clement Watson, Hutton

108 Eric Tattersall, Hutton

109 G. Gilbert, Hutton

110 Marian Roper, Hutton

111 Tom Sefton, Hutton

112 Mr B. W. Fielding, Hutton

113 Michael Edwards, Hutton

114 Dorothy Cowburn, Hutton

115 Mrs Kathleen Crookall, Longton

116 Mr and Mrs S. McLoughlin, Longton

117 Kenneth Braithwaite, Hutton

118 —

119 Marjorie E. Searson, Longton

120 G. M. Mackereth, Hutton

121 Mr and Mrs F. Harwood, Hutton

122 Mr George Ressel, Hutton

123 D. and M. Parkes, Hutton

124 Carole D. Benson, New Longton

125 W. A. Hesketh, Hutton

126 —

127 Mrs P. A. Townson, New Longton

128 Marie I. Lambert, Hutton

129 Thomas J. Preston, Hutton

130 David and Di Barton, Hutton

131 Anthony and Michelle Barton, Hutton

132 A. and E. Sykes, New Longton

133 Jaine and Bryony Hilton-Wellard, Hutton

134 Mrs P. M. Williams, New Longton

135 Roger Little, Longton

136 Mr and Mrs Thomas Broad, Hutton

137 Mr and Mrs P. Owen, Hutton

138 Mr and Mrs R. Kipling, Hutton

139 Mr and Mrs Martin A. H. Wade, Hutton

140 Tom and Bobbie Bretherton, New Longton

141 Miss Kervin, Hutton

142 Bill, Janet and David Craven, Hutton

143   William and Julie Banks, Hutton
144   Mrs S. L. O'Kane, Hutton
145   David Mander, Hutton
146   William and Susan Bradley-White, Hutton